MARGARET RAMSAY LTD

PLAY AGENTS

Margaret Ramsay (Managing Director)
Tom Erhardt (U.S.A.)
William Roderick

Telephone   01 240 0691
              01 836 7403

Cables Ramsayplay London W C 2

14ᴬ Goodwins Court
St Martins Lane
London. WC2N 4LL

Reg Office 99 Aldwych W C 2
Registered in England No 757706

2

If I hadn't heard from you personally, I'd have suggested we sang "Soothe" & thanked you for your endless loyalty & care. If you feel that — you owe me nothing — also, as you owe me nothing — I owe you. You are more f the years associated with your artistic development. You are extraordinary.

But the pressure of the life — the machine — is found & blunt one. It has blunted us all — But it's more serious f a writer of your calibre & I care a great deal that the burden

Peggy Ramsay was the foremost play agent of her time. Born on 27 May 1908 in New South Wales, Australia to English parents, she spent most of her early years in South Africa, where her father converted from Judaism to Christianity. Ramsay went to school in Port Elizabeth and Johannesburg and attended Rhodes University, Grahamstown studying zoology, botany, English, and psychology but left within a year without completing her BSc. She came to England in 1929 and worked as an opera singer and actress before being appointed in 1945 assistant to the director of the newly-formed Bristol Old Vic Theatre. She briefly ran the west London Q Theatre, one of the capital's leading little theatres, and there developed her interest in new plays while demonstrating a rare ability to judge a script on the page. This talent led her to become a play reader for London managements, and in 1953 she was persuaded to open her own playwrights' agency, which became celebrated not just for the range of her clients and the quality of their work but also for her unique relationship with them.

Her list of clients shows her to have been at the centre of British playwriting for several successive generations from the late 1950s on as theatrical taste and conventions changed. She represented leading translators/adaptors, including Barbara Bray, Kenneth Cavander, Michael Meyer, Donald Watson, and Barbara Wright, the stage work of certain prominent novelists, such as Enid Bagnold, Iris Murdoch, J. B. Priestley, Jean Rhys, and Muriel Spark, and a handful of foreign luminaries, such as Arthur Adamov and Eugène Ionesco. At the heart of her work, however, was a dazzling array of new writing talent. Her extensive list included: Rhys Adrian, John Arden and Margaretta D'Arcy, Alan Ayckbourn, Peter Barnes, Robert Bolt, Edward Bond, Howard Brenton, Caryl Churchill, Peter Gill, Steve Gooch, Christopher Hampton, David Hare, Robert Holman, Stephen Jeffreys, Ann Jellicoe, Thomas Kilroy, Henry Livings, Christopher Logue, Stephen Lowe, Frank Marcus, John McGrath, David Mercer, John Mortimer, Peter Nichols, Joe Orton, Alan Plater, Stephen Poliakoff, Jack Rosenthal, David Rudkin, Willy Russell, James Saunders, Wallace Shawn, Martin Sherman, Hugh Whitemore, John Whiting, Charles Wood, and David Wood.

Ramsay has been portrayed in the cinema (by Vanessa Redgrave in the Orton Diaries film *Prick Up Your Ears*) and on stage (as herself, played by Maureen Lipman in Alan Plater's *Peggy for You*, and as inspiration for fictional characters such as Marion in Alan Ayckbourn's *Absurd Person Singular*, Nancy Fraser in Peter Nichols' *A Piece of My Mind*, and Valentina Nrovka in David Hare's *The Bay at Nice*). She has also been the subject of a TV documentary (Arena's *Peggy and Her Playwrights*), a biography (*Peggy: The Life of Margaret Ramsay, Play Agent* by Colin Chambers) and a memoir (*Love Is Where It Falls* by Simon Callow). She is featured in books by and about her clients, and among the plays dedicated to her are Orton's *Loot* and Bond's *The Woman*. In recognition of the wider impact of her writers, the British Film Institute in 1984 gave her an award for her contribution to the film and television industries. She died in London on 4 September 1991.

*

COLIN CHAMBERS, a former journalist and theatre critic, was Literary Manager of the Royal Shakespeare Company (1981–1997), and since 2014 has been Emeritus Professor of Drama at Kingston University. He is co-author with Richard Nelson of *Kenneth's First Play* and *Tynan* (both produced by the Royal Shakespeare Company). He adapted with Steven Pimlott, Molière's *The Learned Ladies* (The Other Place, Stratford-upon-Avon), he selected and edited for performance *Three Farces* by John Maddison Morton (Orange Tree Theatre, Richmond), and he adapted David Pinski's *Treasure* (Finborough Theatre, London). He edited *Making Plays: The Writer-Director Relationship in the Theatre Today* by Richard Nelson and David Jones, co-edited with Richard Nelson *Granville Barker on Theatre*, and edited and contributed to the *Continuum Companion to Twentieth Century Theatre*. He has written extensively on the theatre, including the books *Other Spaces: New Writing and the RSC; Playwrights' Progress* (with Michael Prior); *The Story of Unity Theatre; Peggy: the Life of Margaret Ramsay, Play Agent* (winner of the inaugural Theatre Book Prize); *Inside the Royal Shakespeare Company; Here We Stand: Politics, Performers and Performance – Paul Robeson, Isadora Duncan and Charlie Chaplin; and Black and Asian Theatre in Britain: A History*.

Peggy to her Playwrights

The Letters of
Margaret Ramsay, Play Agent

INTRODUCTION BY SIMON CALLOW

SELECTED AND EDITED BY COLIN CHAMBERS

OBERON BOOKS
LONDON

WWW.OBERONBOOKS.COM

First published in 2018 by Oberon Books Ltd
521 Caledonian Road, London N7 9RH
Tel: +44 (0) 20 7607 3637 / Fax: +44 (0) 20 7607 3629
e-mail: info@oberonbooks.com
www.oberonbooks.com

HB ISBN: 9781786824295
E ISBN: 9781786824301

Cover image by Chris Harris

Printed and bound by CPI Group (UK) Ltd, Croydon, CR0 4YY
eBook conversion by Lapiz Digital Services, India.

To Tom Erhardt

Peggy Ramsay's indefatigable assistant
for twenty years and guardian of her legacy

ACKNOWLEDGEMENTS

*

Thanks are due to Neil Adleman of the Peggy Ramsay Foundation, David Hare, Suzanne Lazenbury, Jane Noble, Trevor Nunn, Garry O'Connor, the Borthwick Institute for Archives (University of York), the Oxfordshire History Centre, the Harry Ransom Center, Austin, Texas, Special Collections (Joe Orton Collection) at the University of Leicester, the Victoria and Albert Theatre & Performance Collections, the staff at Casarotto Ramsay (the agency formed after Ramsay's death), and, despite the onerous request and supply system at the British Library, the staff there who helped me work my way through the Peggy Ramsay Archive. Special thanks are due to Simon Callow, without whom this book would not have happened.

*

Peggy Ramsay believed the living playwright belonged at the centre of theatre and that a theatre without new writing to refresh it was worthless. When she died in 1991 her estate was left for charitable purposes to help writers and writing for the stage. The Peggy Ramsay Foundation was established to further this aim. The Foundation seeks to perpetuate her ideals, by directly helping dramatists at different stages of their experience in order to afford them the time and the space to write. To contact the Foundation, visit http://www.peggyramsayfoundation.org. It only supports writers resident in the British Isles.

CONTENTS

*

The Antennae of Recognition

I was nineteen years old when I first encountered Peggy Ramsay. I was at University in Belfast; during a vacation I had been bowled over by Peter Barnes' neo-Jacobean masterpiece *The Ruling Class* in the West End and wrote to Margaret Ramsay Ltd to ask whether it would be possible, for me to do a production of the play with the Student Drama Society. A letter came hurtling back by return of post, severely berating me for imagining that a highly successful West End play would be available for <u>Amateur Rights</u> (heavily and contemptuously underlined). Repertory Rights would of course precede those, after which, possibly, my request might be considered. The letter was signed, as if in angry haste, Peggy Ramsay. I had been secretly planning to run away from University to become an actor at the end of my first year; this was to be my glorious Swansong. Not, I clearly saw, if the peremptory Miss Ramsay was to have anything to do with it. Better think of something else. And then, a mere day after the first letter came a second. She had spoken to Barnes – just Barnes – about it, she said, and he had very generously decided to allow us to do the play, so I had get better in touch with the office to make the appropriate arrangements.

I didn't. I can't remember why, now – it could have been anything: the cast was too big, there was not enough time to rehearse, people were anxious about various profanities in the text ('I love you from the bottom of my heart to the tip of my penis', that sort of thing) – and I left Belfast to go back to work in Box Offices, there to plot my admission to Drama School. But I had taken away from my brief epistolary encounter with Peggy Ramsay a powerful impression of a woman who was simultaneously mercurial, severe and bossy, but not inflexible: she had, after all, spoken to 'Barnes' and allowed herself to be overruled by him.

I was scarcely to know then that I would in time be the recipient of literally hundreds of letters from Peggy. We met in 1979, ten years after I had first written to her, and we almost immediately fell into a passionate friendship which lasted till the day she died. She was seventy, I was thirty.

We had meals, we went to see plays and to hear music, we frequented art galleries and museums; we talked and talked; our lives became inextricably interwoven. And during all that time, after I had left Peggy back at her flat, and we had said good night to each other, we would continue our friendship in letters. Our relationship had started with them, and so it continued – letters of advice, admonition, tenderness, reproach, inspiration, anger, wisdom. I had never experienced anything like it. If Peggy was incandescent in the flesh – and she was – she was electrifying on the page. Sometimes the letters were concise, sometimes they went on at great length; there could be ten or twelve pages, filled with quotations and sharp analysis. But they were always ablaze, from beginning to end, written at high speed and with surging passion. Above all, they were affirmations of her essential belief: that life was a tremendous test that had to be faced, fearlessly – ferociously, even – and on one's own.

I have never known another human being so fundamentally alone. There was, in the end, no respite for her from this tremendous sense of solitude: her feelings for me, intense as they were, gave her the consolation of meeting a kindred spirit along the way, swapping stories of the journey, its hazards and its accidental splendours, knowing that we would inevitably part, and she that would be back on her way again, sooner or later, alone once more. Her feelings for her companion of twenty-five years, Bill, were vaguely affectionate and kindly, as if he were not so much a partner as a needy relative, though in quite what way they were related, she seemed to have forgotten. He was a lodger, not just in her flat, but in her life. Her feelings for her fellow human beings were less particular, more universal. She was filled with compassion for them, simply because they were human beings, and therefore doomed to disappointment; she even felt acute sympathy for her cat – not love, not tenderness, not affection: pity. It was an essentially tragic view of life, one which she embraced unreservedly, even gleefully, as if she were sailing though a storm at the prow of her ship, the spume splashing her face and the waves threatening to engulf her at any moment.

It made her extraordinary enough as a person, but as an agent, entirely unique. In her dealings with producers and managers, she relished the cut and thrust of negotiations, and was immensely skilful at framing contracts, but she was always pursuing a higher agenda, serving not just writing, or the theatre, but life itself. Mediocrity of spirit was the eternal enemy, in managements and directors and performers, but in her clients, too – 'the authors', as she called them, caressing the word ominously as she said it: it was a high calling, she seemed to say, with attendant obligations. The fact that she almost invariably referred to them by their last names put them among the immortals. She viewed them, on the whole, with deep admiration – they were doing something she couldn't – mingled with watchful vigilance and not a little exasperation. And they viewed encounters with her as bracing but potentially painful, because she could be relied upon to speak her thoughts unmodified by tact or conventional softeners. These meetings had something of the character of a tutorial. She had thought long and deep about what a play was, reading far and wide in dramatic theory, from Aristotle to Brecht; she had studied the lives of dramatists and what they had said about their work. After she died, I found in her flat, hidden away behind the bookshelves, three notebooks, in which she had neatly and diligently transcribed the insights she had gleaned from her reading. Some of these axioms would emerge in her conversations with her clients, but she had long ago consigned them to her subconscious so that nothing would come between the play she was reading or seeing and her intuition, the promptings of which she would then convey as directly as possible to the author. Her analysis of the work in question tended to lead inexorably to a consideration of the author's entire approach to life. She would impart these reflections kindly, even tenderly. This perhaps augmented their shocking impact – that, and the fact that she was a very attractive, sexy, exquisitely dressed woman, with a highly developed, if wild, sense of humour. Sometimes she would chortle at the harshness of the verdicts she was delivering. Authors would leave Peggy's office like drowning men and women, their entire lives up to that point passing before their eyes.

I was not an author when we met, though I had some shy ambitions to be a writer. I was starting to pen occasional pieces for the newspapers, which she cheerfully tore to shreds. 'Why is it so boring?' she would enquire pleasantly. 'Do you intend it to be boring?' Nonetheless, and with some misgivings, she submitted a long talk I had given somewhere to the publisher Nick Hern, and he commissioned a book from me, thus setting me on the path. But, though she always took an interest in my writing, I was not quite an *author* to her. I only wrote prose, and only non-fiction; her special sphere was the drama. She would often share her comments to the authors in her letters to me, and of course I knew she wrote to them all the time. Sometimes playwrights I knew would show me letters they had received from her; they were pretty hair-raising. It was clear that she was judging their work by the highest standards – as often as not, those of the novelists she adored: Balzac, Maupassant, Proust, Thomas Mann, Stefan Zweig; among playwrights, Ibsen and Strindberg were often cited, too. The classics – Shakespeare, Molière, Racine – were less often cited. Her sensibility was essentially modern and European, though her upbringing was African; along with the rigour and dedication that she expected of herself and her authors, there was a wildness of spirit in her, 'due, I think,' she wrote to Edward Bond, 'to having been brought up in countries with wide landscapes, cruel colours, brutal draughts, the whole indifference of nature set before my eyes. It's like expecting a wild cat to live in a suburban house and not claw the furniture and tear up the curtains!'

I tried to convey some of this in *Love Is Where It Falls*, the book I wrote about our friendship; and Colin Chambers in his fine biography, working on a much broader canvas, recounted the whole extraordinary story of her life and career. It was Willy Russell who suggested to me, after the publication of my book, that what was really needed now was a collection of her letters to the authors. I agreed, wholeheartedly. That was nearly twenty years ago. I feel rather embarrassed that it's taken so long, but it could scarcely be more timely. The world has turned upside down in that time, as has the theatre. New values have prevailed, new expectations been aroused, new lines drawn in the sand. What Peggy would have made of any of this can be readily guessed: she would have fought like a tiger for the primacy of the playwright and demanded more rigour – and more wildness – from everyone concerned: managers, directors, performers, authors. But the voice that is to be heard in these letters, though distinctly of its period, both in tone and in intellectual framework, has a remarkable, almost timeless, authority, appealing as it does to eternal verities – not as the basis of rules or prescriptions, but as the ultimate source of living art.

When Colin Chambers first delivered his selection of letters, even I, deeply familiar with Peggy's epistolary manner as I was, was taken aback.

They cover a variety of aspects of her work as an agent (a word, incidentally, that she despised): here we find her, for example, arranging a holiday for an exhausted Alan Ayckbourn, there advising an asthmatic David Hare to take Alexander classes. But again and again, dealing with the everyday business of getting plays commissioned, produced and performed, she elevates the entire enterprise to another level. Without being in the least pompous or sententious, she keeps taking things back to first principles. Her letter to Edward Bond, then a new client, in which she describes her work, is astonishing in its vision of how she sees her calling: 'in itself it requires the almost impossible from anyone who decides to do this job.' From her account of her own work, she does not in the least exaggerate. She was – as we discover elsewhere, in a letter to Enid Bagnold, for example – a martyr to her job, putting in hours and making sacrifices which far exceed anything that might reasonably be expected. But at the same time, leading this circumscribed existence, she contrived to intensify her personality. Significantly, the letter she wrote to Bond about what she did starts with an account of Diaghilev which stresses how hard he worked to serve the talent he unearthed or convoked. Work, not brilliance, was for her the key to his success. That and his devotion to the new – not because he loved it, but simply because it was new, alive, dangerous, difficult. 'Can't you invent some new form, some new language, some new area?' she writes to the radio writer Rhys Adrian. 'Perhaps I should take a single ticket to the moon and start an agency there!'

In fact, she started being an agent – in 1953 – just when the theatre was about to enter one of its periodic phases of renewal. This was not immediately evident at the time; 1953 looked like a very stagnant period, with a number of large and familiar fishes filling a rather small pond. There was no Royal Shakespeare Company and no National Theatre; the English Stage Company had not yet set up shop at the Royal Court. The Arts Theatre and the Gate Theatre were among the handful of theatres largely concerned with new plays, as was the theatre Peggy had briefly run – Q Theatre in Brentford. Joan Littlewood had just established Theatre Workshop at the Theatre Royal Stratford East, which was committed to a new approach to working on plays, but at the start was largely concerned with classics. The Old Vic Theatre never performed new plays. There was vigorous commitment to new writing in repertory theatres across the country; the West End, too, was by no means devoid of new writing, technically speaking, by figures as distinguished as Terence Rattigan, T. S. Eliot, Christopher Fry and Graham Greene, but, as Kenneth Tynan gloomily remarked in 1954, 'the bare fact is that, apart from revivals and imports, there is nothing in the London theatre that one dares to discuss with an intelligent man for more than five minutes.' The theatre was controlled by managers who shrewdly gauged the taste of their audiences, who were for the most part consisted of the well-heeled middle classes. These managers' theatres were well-run, their actors were well-mannered, their plays were well-made, and within those parameters the West End was a pillar of good taste and impeccable standards. But it excluded experiment, imagination, unbuttoned emotion – and the working classes.

All that was about to change. But at the beginning of her career (another word she despised), Peggy was dealing with the grandees of the business. And, typically, she rather liked them, though everything they stood for was inimical to her view both of life and of art. In particular, she warmed to Hugh 'Binkie' Beaumont, the arch-grandee, 'because loyalty is the keystone to his character, and love for people, absurd people, who gossip and love and slip up and so forth. Utterly 'human', as she wrote to her client Robert Bolt. Binkie liked Peggy too, valuing her judgement and finding her, as she was, wonderful company. But she tired of the social round soon enough. 'Those long smoky drinky evenings with Binkie, when he plots away trying to manipulate the theatre,' as she wrote to Joe Orton. 'They always amuse and interest me, but don't finally give one anything but a bad night's sleep.' Large shifts were occurring in the theatre which would soon leave Binkie and his fellow managers isolated from the vital currents of theatrical life.

She was now dealing with a quite different group of people, the ones who were making the running, many of them a good twenty years younger than she was: twenty-four-year-old Peter Hall, fresh from the Oxford Playhouse, now in charge of the Arts, where, right in the heart of the West End, he presented a remarkably challenging season, culminating in *Waiting for Godot*; the rising young producer, Michael Codron, and George Devine, her contemporary, at the head of a talented and opinionated group of young directors who formed the English Stage Company at the Royal Court

Theatre. She did everything she could to encourage them, sending them the work of her also increasingly younger list of writers, writing directly to critics both before and after the opening of her authors' plays to draw their attention to what she thought was important work, or a startling new voice, asserting her entrenched conviction that what is genuinely new always appears ugly at first until we understand its language. She did not limit the communication of these observations to reviewers of her own authors: in the case of both Beckett and Pinter, for instance, neither of whom she ever represented, she wrote to Harold Hobson, the powerful critic of the London *Sunday Times*, to urge the respective merits of *Godot* and *The Birthday Party*.

And while she was tirelessly urging directors and producers to put on her authors' work, and badgering critics to make sure that they understood its merits, and securing the possible financial deals for them, she was warning them about 'success (the killer)', as she called it, breeding, as she felt it did, greed and laziness and disconnecting the authors from the sources of their talent. Robert Bolt was a particular focus of her concerns: he was the first client she brought on from nowhere – she had been shown a play of his which she was certain had promise and worked tirelessly to ensure that it was done and done well; then she fought hard to keep him on the straight and narrow, though his inclinations were wayward: 'Bolt could become one of the big playwrights, if he learns, develops, and <u>survives</u>.' As she urged him to make sacrifices: 'I mean that you shouldn't allow yourself any of the indulgences that success and money have brought. NO "living it up", no escapes to grand hotels, no "special benefits" …. I am very serious about this. You must live exactly as your audience lives, with all the concerns which we have all the time. I am certain that this is essential if you are to write a play which is to strike us bang in the middle.' This is what, in one form or another, she urged on all her authors. When David Mercer declared his intention of going to live in Israel, Peggy wrote: 'You could only live there if the theatre really doesn't matter to you. It's not missing interviews with these top Directors which is the main problem. It's keeping out of touch with the collective subconscious of England. Love, Peggy.'

It was not just her clients. She had a beady eye on Peter Hall, now ensconced at the head of the company he founded, the RSC:

'This man Hall had a marvellous creative talent, he was way ahead of everyone, he did remarkable things because of the necessities of his talent to create. We now have a great powerful figure, one of the few to emerge at the top of the tree – but we have lost the remarkable, selfless creative human being – the person who operated alone, and who changed our theatre by his single talent.'

No one was spared her strictures; her courage was limitless. She wrote to Laurence Olivier, whom she barely knew, asking him to release Bolt from a commitment to translate Ibsen's *The Pretenders*. As usual, she decided that telling the truth was the best policy.

'When two of his most recent pieces of work are, to my mind, sub-standard, obviously it is my job as his agent to say so, loud and clear. As soon as Bob arrived off the plane, I had a very serious talk to him, and explained to him that unless he was to be a dedicated writer, rather than a merely professional writer, then he would quite soon become a hack. (I don't have to explain to you what I mean by a "dedicated" person towards their job because you afford the perfect example of such a person).'

When she felt that Bolt's 1958 play *Flowering Cherry* was falling short, on tour, of what it might be, notably in the area of emotion, she wrote the director, Frith Banbury, a serious and outstandingly skilful director, an altogether extraordinary letter, in which she quotes, sometimes at considerable length, Maupassant, Quiller-Couch, Baudelaire, Havelock Ellis, Ovid, Gide, D. H. Lawrence, Racine and Villon, many of them in the original language. She calculated (not incorrectly) that Banbury, unlike many another director of the time, would be swayed by an appeal to the literary masters of high feeling. A play was never just a play, an author was not just an author: both had the possibility of transcending themselves, and must be given every chance to do so. And that always meant going back to first principles. In this case, it seems to have worked: the play was acclaimed as a British *Death of a Salesman* and had a long run in the West End; it launched Bolt's career.

Unquestionably, the most extraordinary professional relationship she had was with Joe Orton, who in many ways was for her the *beau idéal* of what a writer should be in his independence, simplicity of life and failure to be seduced by the world of the theatre or the blandishments of fame.

She even admired what she saw as his growing indifference to writing; like Rimbaud, she felt, he had used art for as long as it was useful to him and then cast it aside. Her letter describing him to Harold Hobson in advance of the first production of *Entertaining Mr Sloane* betrays some of her astonishment at meeting someone who behaved exactly as she believed a writer should behave. She had warned Orton, she told Hobson, that she might not try to sell *Sloane* because the critics could perhaps say that it was excessively Pinterish. 'He replied that I must do anything I wished and that he could easily manage if I didn't sell it, because he was living on £3.10.0d p.w. National Assistance, and had been doing so "ever since he came out".' Orton had then gone on to tell her that he had been six months in Wormwood Scrubs for a series of minor thefts and that it had been remarkably good for him. 'When I asked if he intended going back to crime, he said certainly not, if it was possible to earn his living in any other way...I am much struck with a young man who doesn't want to exploit people, who is prepared to live on £3.10.0d p.w., who doesn't whine, or tell a hard luck tale.' She was particularly keen, she told Hobson, that the play should have a proper showing, and hoped that he would like it. Hobson did as he was told; the play – thanks in part to an infusion of money from, of all people, Terence Rattigan – transferred to the West End and did very well.

Orton was not personally going to be seduced by success (the killer), but Peggy fought hard to preserve the directness and freshness of his work from those who sought to over-decorate it. She fell out with old colleagues like the producer Michael Codron and the director Peter Wood over the first over-larded and over-starry production of *Loot*, which she felt had swamped his unique voice, and made sure that it never came to the West End; instead she supported a much lower-key later production which, with an unknown cast, preserved the play's freshness and directness. It transferred to the Criterion Theatre, where it ran and ran. Just a year after its triumphant opening, Orton was bludgeoned to death by his partner, Ken Halliwell. Peggy slipped into the house while the bodies were still there and was appalled but somehow exalted by what she saw. Their lives were many things, but they were not bourgeois. Unsurprisingly, Peggy was haunted by their story: this was the reality of living a life untempered by convention. Even she wondered whether the price was too high, though she told Orton's biographer, John Lahr, that 'I'm not being sentimental when I say that I'm sure Joe wouldn't in the least mind being killed by Kenneth.' Nor did sentiment lead her to over-value Orton's work. 'I liked him as a person and I liked his plays a great deal. I did not think he was a genius.'

By the 1970s Margaret Ramsay Ltd. boasted a remarkable roster of young Turks: Christopher Hampton, Edward Bond, David Hare, Howard Brenton, David Mercer, Charles Wood, John Arden and Margaretta d'Arcy, and a very young Turk indeed, Stephen Poliakoff, recruited by Peggy when he was still at Westminster School. Many of these authors had their work performed at the Royal Court Theatre, self-styled as the writers' theatre. But was it, actually? 'I do understand how, from your point of view, you feel that the Royal Court is totally committed to the authors,' she wrote to the then artistic director, Max Stafford-Clark. 'From our point of view, and I speak for both myself and my clients, we don't feel the same way.' She was concerned that too often the choice of director and designer, and sometimes actors, was made without the author being consulted or considered. Directors' theatre was utterly inimical to her. She knew whereof she spoke. 'Before I was an Agent I ran a theatre. A mistake over the choice of director, designer, play, actors and lighting was crucial. In fact the major thing I learnt was that a play is a success or failure on the first day of rehearsal, and when one sat in a dress rehearsal a mistake in one of the ingredients simply shattered one.'

A great deal of Peggy's contribution to the process of writing or indeed staging a play came from this practical experience. The letters collected here are full of practical wisdom. A recent and highly regarded textbook about story-telling – *Into the Woods* by John Yorke – approvingly quotes the answer she gave to her client Alan Plater when he asked her for guidance about structure: 'Oh darling,' she said, 'it's just two or three little surprises followed every now and again by a bigger surprise.' All of her clients at one time or another received the recommendation, when they were having difficulties with a scene, to look at the one before, where, she said, the real problem was to be found. She was full of curious knowledge: Peggy on the subject of the Dutch cap in her correspondence with Bernard Miles is eye-opening. Needless to say, she was not always right (although she seems to have been spot-on about the Dutch cap). That was not the point: the point was, as will be very clear from the contents of this book, that she always provoked anyone she came into contact with to think very hard about what they were doing and why.

Above all the letters burst at the seams with her incomparable personality. She wrote as she spoke: to read her correspondence is to be in the room with her again. Her throwaway comments are collectable in themselves – 'you will be surprised how patient provincial audiences are,' she wrote to David Mercer. 'They are quite used to dead actors.' Her anarchism, never far below the surface, rises to the surface from time to time: 'Personally I didn't see ANY Mods or Rockers at Brighton (where she was about to buy a house)', she reported to Charles Wood. 'I must decide which side I'm on by next Bank Holiday so that I too can break up a few deck chairs and do a bit of damage. You and Peter (Nichols) can cheer me on. I'd love to do a bit of destruction and don't really get a proper chance. I DO so sympathise with the kids over this, and think we should have adult factions and go out weekly and bust up districts. Eaton Square, for instance, or Buck House.' Even more alarming, she tells Ayckbourn that murder is a basic part of family life. 'I tried to murder my mother by throwing a hot iron at her, and when I think about the incident I still feel the same rage and dissatisfaction at not having done it. My father knew these intermittent impulses of mine, but took them as casually as your character Edward.' But at root, she was concerned with cultivating an attitude to life. It is this which seems to me to place this collection of her letters in the territory of Rilke's *Letter to A Young Poet*. Like Rilke, in the end she was saying: 'Nobody can advise you and help you, nobody. There is only one way. Go into yourself.'

Somewhere I have a copy of John Osborne's memoir, *A Better Class of Person*. He has inscribed it 'To Peggy: a better class of agent.' She was, in fact, in a class of her own. Producers', directors' and authors' lives are easier now that she's gone.

Alas.

Simon Callow

*

For Peggy Ramsay, playwrights and their art came first, before managers, directors, actors, and even the writers' partners and families. Although Ramsay enjoyed the cut-and-thrust of negotiating and the gamble of the box office, the business side of the firm was secondary. She would turn work down for clients – often without recourse to the playwrights themselves – if she felt it was not right for them. Developing talent was what ignited her, and in her stoical 'tough love' she was a practical yet hard taskmistress.

The telephone was her natural weapon of choice but she was also an energetic correspondent in the era before fax, the internet, email, and social media. Alongside letters dealing with the business side of theatre – inevitably the majority of her output – are letters extending across a marvellous array of topics, both personal and professional. They frequently deal with the interconnection between and interdependence of life and art, and are distinguished by their candour.

Only letters written by Ramsay have been included here. They are organised alphabetically by client, and are followed by a short postscript of letters to non-clients, arranged chronologically, which give a sense of her wider correspondence. Her clients overwhelmingly were playwrights but she also represented novelists who wrote plays or whose work was adapted for the stage, translators and adaptors (some of whom were primarily directors), a few designers, and, in the case of Simon Callow, an actor who wrote. Under individual playwrights are included related letters to non-clients, for example to producers such as Binkie Beaumont and Michael Codron, and to directors such as Frith Banbury, in which she navigates the vicissitudes of her client's work from page to stage.

Most of the originals are typed, including many self-typed in Ramsay's inimitable style, and some are handwritten. Reproducing letters that fall into the latter two categories involves editorial interpretation. This appears in square brackets, as do any explanations, which have been kept to a minimum and are included only for clarity. There are no footnotes but, where necessary, a brief introductory note to set context as well as the biographical dates of the clients around whom the book is organised. Lay out and spelling have been standardised and, to avoid repetition and/or unnecessary detail (e.g. over contractual matters), letters have been edited, sometimes heavily. The self-typed letters have been corrected for ease of reading – Ramsay regularly typed Ive and its without the apostrophes, transposed letters, and mis-spelled names. In one letter to Enid Bagnold, she wrote, 'I see you mention Sybil Thorndike. Do please spell her <u>Dike</u> not dyke!!!' though Ramsay herself had made that same mistake. She used different styles for naming plays and books, and often shortened the names, but these have been left unless intelligibility was compromised. Samples of her typing and handwriting can be found on the endpapers of the book.

This selection represents only a tiny fraction of her correspondence and aims to capture Ramsay's singular spirit and what made her distinctive rather than offer a comprehensive historical account of her work. Inevitably, not all the writers are represented, and, of those that are, the letters that have been chosen do not necessarily or always epitomize her relationship to those playwrights, though some do.

Most of her surviving letters are held in the British Library's Margaret Ramsay archive, which contains 539 client files. These cover some 200 clients and each contains from one to thirty files (Robert Bolt). Her letters are also held in collections of individual writers housed in various institutions, and some are held privately. A few are not available for publication (and in some cases reading) for reasons of confidentiality. Several clients took their letters away from Ramsay. Over the years, she had regular clear-outs and doubtless threw away a number of letters (and claimed to have done this to her correspondence with Samuel Beckett), and an unknown, though probably small, quantity was lost in 1991 in a fire at her office.

Colin Chambers, 2018

ARTHUR ADAMOV

Adamov (1908–1970), an avant-garde writer from Azerbaijan living in France, was little known in Britain in 1959 when he came to Ramsay needing representation for a radio play. He stayed with Ramsay five years during which time he was crowned one of the key writers of the Theatre of the Absurd. Ramsay's Francophone clients also included Fernando Arrabal, Marcel Aymé, Eugène Ionesco, Morvan Lebesque, René de Obaldia, Robert Pinget, Armand Salacrou, and Boris Vian.

30 July 1962

Dear Mr. [*Charles*] Marowitz [*co-founder of* Encore *theatre magazine and a director*],

Many thanks for returning the copies of the Adamov plays. I more than understand the difficulties in launching these plays. We're very grateful to you for trying. He's an altogether admirable man.

The trouble about the "old" Adamov plays is that he has entirely changed his voice, and they appear to be the work of a different author.

I didn't really wholeheartedly like these early plays, yet I miss the freedom and imagination he brought to them. Nowadays he is so determined to <u>teach</u> and <u>record</u>, and one sometimes finds oneself wanting to act like an obstreperous schoolboy and make a disturbance, or behave badly in some way or other – one wants to "blow up" either during, or after, the performance. Is this good?

By the way, I'm a great admirer of your articles, though I don't always agree with you. I also enjoyed what you had to say at a meeting sometime back when you, Bolt (my client), a young American, and a somewhat submerged [*John*] McGrath shared a platform. I told Bob Bolt after the meeting that I'd not agreed with anything <u>at all</u> he'd said on that occasion! On the whole playwrights should be muzzled and prevented from theorising and arguing, as they have a perfectly good outlet of their own. (I've just realised that of course <u>you</u> have this outlet too, yet I'd be disappointed if you confined yourself to it!).

Sincerely yours,

16 October 1962

Dear Arthur Adamov,

I have just telephoned Barbara Bray [*radio producer who introduced Adamov to Ramsay*] to tell you that the Director John Dexter is hoping to come to Paris Monday and Tuesday of next week to meet you. He is an outstandingly good director from the Royal Court and he is entirely responsible for Wesker's success.

Laurence Olivier has asked him to choose and direct a play for next year's Chichester Festival and he is extraordinarily interested in "SPRING'71".

He does not speak French, so I have asked Barbara whether if necessary, she could help Dexter. I have told him you understand English well but it may be possible that he wants to ask you difficult questions and he would be unable to understand your reply. I am giving him your phone number and address in Paris. I think you will like him very much indeed. I do hope we can arrange this production – it would be splendid, don't you think?

Warmest regards,

Ever yours,

RHYS ADRIAN

*

Adrian (1928–1990) joined Ramsay in the 1950s as a radio writer and became a noted radio and television playwright.

Dear Rhys,

What I feel is this: a pessimistic outlook is not an acceptance of despair or defeat, nor is it necessarily destructive; it is merely the way certain people interpret life – your hero did not "opt out" or commit suicide, he went on, knowing that the human conditions were pretty well unendurable.

The letter you received suggested that your play was as if a doctor diagnosed certain symptoms but made no effort, or could not, effect a cure; but surely nobody can offer a <u>solution</u> for living – partial alleviations, perhaps, but there is no formula, alas. If there were, we should all be happy people, and the world would not suffer from wars, starvation and the like.

People seem to think that optimism is right and pessimism wrong – one might just as well lay down the law that only romanticism is permitted, and that nobody should write anything but comedies. Everyone, thank god, is permitted to see life through their own eyes and their own temperaments. Because Schopenhauer is a "pessimist", does not mean that he is a great philosopher, or, in fact, greater than Nietzsche (who was probably the prop and mainstay of Adolph Hitler, who imagined that a "purified race" was the answer to the world's ills, and we all know what misery THAT led to!)

The man who wrote you is the kind of person who is railing against Beckett. Such a man would probably prefer to have no playwright than, say, Ben Travers. Personally I find that a light comedy in the theatre drives me out feeling near suicide, though I have laughed a lot; whereas after something like Oedipus or Hamlet, I feel an exhilaration and a purpose in living.

But it's useless to argue with people who think that one must not face truth and reality, but only accept the gay and the false. There has always been a large body who <u>need</u> "escapist" theatre (and TV), and as life is frankly unbearably harsh, one must try and understand how many people want to run away from the truth and seek comfort in the romantic and idealised. Unfortunately you aren't really writing for these people, so that you must face the fact that you will not get either their support or understanding. However, don't blame them, pity them.

Love,

4 January 1967

My dear Rhys,

Can't you invent some new form, some new language, some new area? Perhaps I should take a single ticket to the moon and start an agency there!

Love,

JOHN ARDEN AND MARGARETTA D'ARCY

*

Arden (1930–2012), already a major writer, and D'Arcy (1934–), his co-author and wife, joined Ramsay in 1967 after their agent had lost his clients' money through speculation. It was a time when Arden and D'Arcy along with many others were re-thinking the role and practice of theatre.

5 May 1967

My dear John and Margaretta,

I have just come back from Bristol where I saw Charles Wood's play DINGO, which is an attack on war. I was tremendously moved by it, though he has about six false endings which sort of dissipate one's passion though each ending is valid. He is in Turkey at the moment, so I can't talk to him. The National had this play but waited for two years, so we took it away from them. The Bristol Arts Centre did it with a few professionals and the rest amateurs – just the kind of set up you like. I thought it was marvellously acted and the attack on war, Montgomery, Churchill, etc. quite alarming, and the Desert Warfare frightening to an extreme. Anyone who sat through that play would never subscribe to war again. This Arts Centre has a theatre, a café, a tiny restaurant in the cellar, and a membership of several thousand, and I do urge you to let them do your plays. I am writing to thank them for last night, and I want to say that I think you would both be pleased to have your work done there.

Of course, everything you say about how you want to work and where you want to work is right. This fetish [?] of success and money is ludicrous. Work must be done for its own sake, and everything one writes should say something which concerns us all. This is what is so marvellous about the possibilities in the theatre today. One doesn't have to be a H.M. Tennent writer and one's ambition needn't be to appear in Shaftesbury Avenue. As for the National and the Aldwych [*the RSC theatre*], the Aldwych is dedicated to the glory of Peter Hall, and the National governed by a Board, and I don't honestly trust Ken [*Tynan*] finally, and Olivier is one of those middle-class middle-brow people we talked about when we met once. I haven't any further time to write, but I am delighted to hear that you are coming back [*from New York*] in June – we can then talk fully.

No more for the moment.

Love to you both,

2 October 1968

Dear John and Margaretta,

I have been wanting to organise somewhere for us to meet this week, but I'm quite exhausted with appointments and just don't know how to make this possible.

Last night I went to a dress rehearsal of [*David*] Cregan's play and had five minutes to rush to a TV set to see another author's 10.30 p.m. TV play. Tonight I have to go to a Gandhi Prayer Meeting and then rush back to see another TV play. I have a meeting with lawyers tomorrow followed by another TV play and I want to escape to Brighton on Friday loaded with scripts.

I don't honestly understand why all of us are so hopelessly bogged down by work; I mean those of us who aren't creative. It's perfectly ridiculous that we're like this and that we can never get a moment of pleasure. It seems to me that we must organise things very badly indeed, as we're certainly not so important this this stupid cluttering of our time is justified. I do hope that rehearsals are going well.

Love,

25 August 1969

Dear Mr. Savory [*Head of Plays, BBC*],

I realise that an agent and the Head of Drama must approach problems of plays from opposite sides, and possibly my feelings may therefore seem to you irrelevant or impractical for your purposes.

Those of us who look after authors, live by virtue of their talents, and talent is, therefore, our livelihood. It is also the livelihood of the BBC.

I don't find either John or Margaretta "easy" and although I occasionally try and talk to them practically I never really expect them to listen, because basically I know that Arden has the finest talent writing in England today and possibly in the English speaking world and I think perhaps he has been denied the view from the <u>other</u> end of the microscope. Talent of this order isn't a convenient or comfortable thing, and unfortunately requires an enormous amount of work and understanding from other people.

When this project [*a trilogy that became* The Island of the Mighty] was commissioned, it was two and a half years ago, and costs were not so high, and the BBC wasn't putting cost before talent, or good plays before "ratings". Bakewell [*previous Head of Plays*] was warned by John that this would be costly, but encouraged him to proceed. I myself wasn't privileged to look after John at the time, or I could have warned him.

The change of attitude in two and a half years in <u>all</u> TV has been astonishing – as astonishing as the great number of shattering events which have taken place during that time. You have to steer the Drama department of your great organisation within this new frame, and I realise how difficult and what a strain it must be. But surely, if the BBC, or TV altogether, is not to become the mediocre matter which the once remarkable American TV has now become – it is essential that occasionally there must be some play or programme of extraordinary merit, costly though it may be. There are thousands of professional playwrights who are turning out workmanlike budgetable plays, which will go on and be forgotten the next morning.

I don't think the Arden trilogy is in this category <u>at all</u>, so that I don't think the ordinary professional rules of budgeting can be applied. Nobody would expect the BBC to spend £100,000, yet I don't think this <u>need</u> cost anything like this amount. It requires the kind of matching talent which can meet John's, and somehow put on the plays within a budget which <u>could</u> be afforded. If a theatre Manager were to get a play like THE TEMPEST in a manuscript in 1969, he might well say that it couldn't be put on for £100,000, but he would be wrong, because it can, and we know that it can. (Would the TEMPEST cost TV £100,000 by the way? Surely not?)

My feelings are, therefore, that a way HAS to be found, every now and then, for something that doesn't obey the rules. I know that John doesn't demand thousands of pounds spending on what he writes. Couldn't someone from the BBC, wanting to direct it, talk over these problems with John with love and admiration and see whether it is really necessary to spend as much as the budget-department has assessed? I think the BBC needs John more than John needs the BBC. I am not talking as an agent, but as somebody who still thinks TV is marvellous and longs to continue to be able to be proud of what we can do with it over here. It CAN'T be impossible, if one can try hard enough to find a way can it?

Sincerely yours,

1 July 1970

My dear John and Margaretta,

Thank you for your letter of June 23. All we received was the second cable saying everything was fine, which was very puzzling and disturbing, as you casually mentioned being held by the police in the last letter we received [*from Assam, northeast India*]. I'll pass your note on to Paul so he can have plenty of time to transfer £1,000 to National and Grindlay's Bank, Connaught Place, New Delhi, and I hope you'll pick up a copy of this letter when you arrive there on July 21.

Do be careful about going through your money too lavishly. I'm a bit worried that you'll be without sufficient means when you return. However, I don't know exactly what you have in the bank, but I'm sure Paul does, and you probably do too. Take care of yourselves and realise that money is merely a way of taking care of yourselves and keeping off the pressure.

Please let me know if you'd like us to get in touch with someone in New Delhi, i.e. perhaps we could ask lawyers, accountants, etc. whether they know some powerful gentleman there who might be of help. I hope you're carrying around a set of your plays in hard-back to dazzle everyone. But maybe they are frightened of the written word and intellectuals!

Please let us know when you get to New Delhi whether you have received the money and the letter all right.

You seem to be putting your drama into your lives, not into your plays my dear John and Margaretta.

Much love to you both,

PS. How are the children faring? How they must long for a semi-detached bourgeois existence with Coronation Street on every evening at 7.30 p.m. (There was a Granada strike and I understand the country was deprived of Coronation Street for some weeks, but of course they're back again.)

[undated, August 1971]

My dear Margaretta and John,

How pleasant to hear from you both. One's life is in constant danger because of <u>other people's</u> driving. Thank god for your armour plated vehicle. I would indeed love to nip up to see you all. We've got a certain amount of necessary visiting vis a vis try outs during the next few weeks, but maybe it might be possible to escape – how sweet of you to suggest it.

We've been having a difficult birth for Mortimer's little TV play VOYAGE ROUND MY FATHER, which opened last week with Guinness at the

Haymarket. The play was earlier tried out at Greenwich, with the TV cast. Two young men paid £2500 which just covered the set.

The play, with Mark Dignam, got splendid notices, but the boys couldn't even pay the £2500, far less persuade any backers to give another £15,000. Everything was therefore abandoned and several months later Guinness asked to do it, the Haymarket offered its stage and Codron presented it.

But success has left me with many heart-searchings: what kind of theatre are we promoting? Should I not have insisted that Dignam should have done the part, and to hell with Guinness. In fact, I just didn't think. And one should think. The West End is crammed with deplorable plays, led by so called stars, and now it's becoming impossible to do ANY plays without stars – and that goes for the Royal Court too, who are the worst of the lot. I saw a run through of part of Osborne's [West of Suez] and [Ralph] Richardson is playing a "writer". What kind of writer I asked [Anthony] Page [the director] – oh, any writer; he stands I suppose for England, says Anthony. But, in fact, Richardson is playing Richardson, having trouble with his lines – he's no writer I've ever imagined on land or sea. But it insures a transfer.

I've written Michael [Codron] that we have GOT to find an excellent play with an excellent part, and give it to Mark and run it. We have GOT to stop this insidious tendency for the author now to be less important than the star. Time was when an author could command a theatre – what has happened? What has gone wrong? I am deeply concerned, and feel that I too have been dreamy and careless and indifferent, or lazy or disenchanted with the theatre (and you can say THAT again!).

I've got a pamphlet about the Common Market put out by the Government, in my flat. I'll bring it back tomorrow and post it off to you.

I've just had a phone message from Page asking me to go to the Court tonight to see the Osborne (still at the preview stage). He says the last scene doesn't work. I've replied that a cliché suggestion is that maybe it's not been prepared for. I've often found that when one scene proves difficult or unintelligible, it's worth looking at the scene which precedes it (can I hear John laughing? Is this very naive?).

Love to you all,

P.S. The Managers West End Contracts: Well I don't remember if I told you there was an assembly of a dozen or so agents. We all condemned the Managers Draft. But a lot of nonsense was also spoken – like Harvey Unna saying that we have to insist that the Managers don't take off a play until they are losing money. My reply to that was we were telling Managers to leave authors alone and merely get their share, so I didn't think we could demand a control of their productions. Managers don't as a rule take off plays if they are making money anyway.

We made a lot of suggestions, and some of the agents – those who love committees – were going to draft an <u>author's</u> contract. I've not seen it, or heard anything more. Meanwhile we've had to sell one or two plays to the very ringleaders. I've taken their Draft, and based a proper contract on their format – changing nearly every clause. They can take it or leave it. They will in fact take it. I don't think an Authors contract is likely to solve everything. It must still be negotiated play by play. And I doubt if you can stop the worst of the West End Managers, who are making a fortune from trippers at the moment. A deplorable little piece called NO SEX PLEASE WE'RE BRITISH is taking over £7000 p.w., I'm told.

Bond's LEAR is in rehearsal. I'll send you the notice etc., as I know you'll be interested. For the rest, it's dog days in the theatre at present. And a near collapse of the film industry.

2 August 1971

Dear Margaretta,

This isn't an easy letter to write, but it would seem to me to be dishonest of me not to report to you one of the problems of setting up an Arden play at the present time.

It seems that <u>you</u> have put the fear of hell into some of the Managers – probably due to that exasperating clash with the ICA [*over the venue for the Arden/D'Arcy melodrama* The Hero Rises Up] – I don't know.

I had a letter from the Royal Court which intimated that they didn't want to revive an Arden play if you were likely to come to rehearsals. This attitude could affect the new play, too, by the way.

I KNOW it's absurd, but people are just not capable of having the truth told to them bang off – I know that I am always in trouble because I say exactly what I mean, and take it for granted that where a play is concerned it is the play that matters, and one can't just remain silent while it is being bitched up. (I am at the moment in trouble for having dropped a note to the Director of the Mortimer play, which I thought was a mere pointing out of some of the points he missed and which really HAD to be considered!)

As soon as David Jones returns from his hols I will have a talk to him about the new play [The Island of the Mighty]. The Aldwych, I am sure, have no "fear" of you, it's merely a matter of getting Jones aside for a moment to tell me exactly what they think about whether they will do it or not.

Warm regards to all of you,

Arden and D'Arcy went on strike when the director David Jones refused to let them address a company meeting to air their criticisms of the Royal Shakespeare Company production of The Island of the Mighty.

27 November 1972

Dear David [*Jones*],

I have received a copy of your letter to the Ardens dated the 24th November. What a pity you did not write this to them on Monday night after Margaretta had seen the play and made the request that there should be a full meeting.

You called on me to tell me what happened. You did not during that meeting point out that of course you did not deny the authors the right to call a meeting. That was what they had asked for, and if you had agreed to it, I would have passed this on to them immediately.

However, I did not in any way try and fan the flames, or put further obstacles between you, as my whole concern was to have rehearsals resume on a collaborative footing.

I did not phone you again, because you asked me to phone the following night, and by that time the Ardens had informed me to do nothing as they were on strike. They did not consult me about this move – they informed me. I have not seen them in person since.

As for the strange story which came from the actors to the authors that I have now "retracted" – I do not understand. Retracted <u>what</u>? I am not at all happy that you are somehow dragging me into this and somehow suggesting that I exaggerated our meeting or deliberately distorted it for some kind of evil or wicked reason. WHY SHOULD I DO THIS? All my interests are for a smooth relationship between you all, and that fruitful rehearsals should resume.

I have been cool and apart from the start, and am a very minor actor in this drama. It would be monstrous and illogical that any suggestion should be made that I played any part which was NOT for the good of the play and the production.

During all the years I have been an agent I have never made trouble between Manager and authors. I do not go in for trouble making so why should I start now? Nor do I think that you could find anybody who would say that I have ever told a deliberate lie.

Sincerely yours,

Ramsay's office became the headquarters of the campaign to support Arden and D'Arcy. Despite her private reservations, she helped with legal advice, rallied support, and took hot soup to the picket line.

13 December 1972

Dear Bob [*Bolt*],

David Jones (or his theatre) sent me a copy of the letter he wrote you dated the 12 December. I am puzzled by it.

When Jones came to the office immediately after his meeting with the Ardens, he told me Margaretta had screamed at him and been entirely destructive of <u>everything</u>. Margaretta certainly said that perhaps the best thing that could happen would be for them to return to Ireland, and I wish to God they <u>had</u> gone, but you couldn't have dragged Margaretta out of England as she smelt blood.

David actually said that he had been <u>very</u> upset by Margaretta and hoped they <u>would</u> return to Ireland immediately, <u>because he could not agree to an immediate meeting of everyone</u>, but if he were left alone he might just possibly be able to get the play on the stage on his own terms by the opening. I felt quite sympathetic to his point raised.

The trouble about David is that he hasn't the guts to stand by what he said, i.e. that he wouldn't let the Ardens talk to the full assembly the day after they had seen the show because it would have demoralised the cast.

<u>Every one</u> of the Aldwych staff – particularly Trevor Nunn [*RSC Artistic Director*] – banned the Ardens who were, I imagine distraught and behaved badly. But the ugly implication of it all is that he left the Ardens quite happy after the run-through, came to me, <u>and what I reported to the Ardens somehow led them into an immediate strike.</u> This is so despicable and fantastic that I don't quite know how to proceed.

My own opinion is that David was scared to death of getting the play on at all, wanted to protect the whole company from a scene, and the Ardens' mad action in making the affair "political" got the incident totally out of hand. If they had not "struck" and had not "withdrawn their labour" the whole thing might have sorted itself out.

Love,

26 January 1973

Dear John and Margaretta,

I saw the play on Wednesday. I was dreading seeing it, but I must confess I was transported by the play, and it wasn't even spoiled by the way it was done. Of course I disliked [*her client*] Tim [*O'Brien*]'s drop cloths – I thought they were wrong and in no way suited the very interesting basic stage set. The theatre was nearly empty, and the actors were adequate without being remarkable. I think the music had nothing much to do with the play. The tragedy is that everything should have been worked together – I hadn't realized before that a bourgeois theatre like the RSC is hopeless. They are striving to appear contemporary and left-wing; it's ridiculous, they ought to do the well-made classic in conventional style.

But this does not affect the value of the plays. I was perhaps most drawn by the second, because of its delectable lyricism, but all of them are marvellous in themselves and I enjoyed them and admired them greatly.

Of course the scandal must die down in England before we can get a proper production, but it is obviously essential that Methuen bring out a definitive text, because the play will be available for the future.

The political front is extraordinary here. Yesterday [*Milton*] Shulman quite casually wrote an article suggesting that capitalism could collapse. I suspect his object lesson was to point out to the TUC and to the "workers" who he thinks want an adjusted capitalism, and not a destruction of capitalism!

It seems over here as if the Americans are pulling out of Vietnam because the country has insisted upon this and Nixon has finally got to do this, but it sounds as if the war is going to go on in exactly the same way and that Nixon is talking about the end of the war whereas he should simply be saying he is being forced to pull out. It all seems quite disgusting.

Flu is raging in London and we have all got heavy colds so are not thinking too clearly. I therefore hope this letter makes some sense.

Love,

ALAN AYCKBOURN

*

The manager Peter Bridge bought the rights to Ayckbourn's early play Standing Room Only, *which had appeared at the Library Theatre, Scarborough in 1961 under the pseudonym Roland Allen. Ayckbourn (1939–), then an actor at the Library Theatre, did not have an agent, and Bridge sent the play to Ramsay. Ayckbourn stayed with Ramsay until her death.*

Dear Alan,

I really loved Act I, but honestly, it is beyond the bounds of possibility to keep up the standard of this play for three acts if it is to remain all the time on the bus. My spirits began flagging badly in Act II and III, and I would give the world for Act II to be set elsewhere, i.e. say, the bar of the Globe Theatre.

You need a long sustaining scene to act as contrast between Act I and III, and you can't possibly do anything but short choppy scenes if you remain on the bus. While I was reading Act II I thought about this, and wondered whether it would be possible to have a party in Act II set in the Globe bar, but then I found you had decided to give a party in Act III.

I know this is a very drastic suggestion, and one which would be appalling hard work for you, and probably unacceptable to Bridge. However, I feel I must make it, because I don't think it is humanly possible to maintain our interests throughout the play with the limitations with the set imposed upon you.

The important thing about this play is that it is a really tremendously good idea, and it is essential that <u>all</u> the acts must be equally entertaining. It is a fatal thing for a play to have the first act as the best one.

Perhaps I am wrong about this, and I would very much like to be persuaded that I am.

Yours ever,

28 March 1962

Dear Alan,

Delighted to get your letter – I'm really so divorced with what is going on that I can't really put in a useful spoke. However, the version <u>I</u> read will be difficult to sustain the whole evening, I <u>think</u>. I said the same thing to Ann Jellicoe, however, and I don't know whether I was right or wrong, and the notices are so different that clearly it's a matter of opinion. I suppose that I underrate the attention that the public are prepared to pay in the commercial theatre, and therefore think they need to be helped with changes of mood, rhythm, and even scenes. (I'm still childish enough to groan when the same set appears act after act! – I long for it to be turned round, or put upside down – <u>something</u>!!!!!)

There is no doubt at all, however, that you have a very great deal of talent and that much of the play is quite tremendously funny. I've never found before that I've been incapable of judging a play by reading it – if I couldn't do this I'd very quickly starve, since its by judging a script that I sell a play as a rule. What <u>can't</u> be proved is when one is <u>entirely</u> right or <u>entirely</u> wrong. There is no way telling whether, in fact, a play could have been much better by doing so and so. Ann Jellicoe withdrew THE KNACK because she thought Keith Johnstone [*the director*] and the actors hadn't done it justice – my complaint was always with the script. Now she has a new production, new actors and a slightly better script – but today she told me that she thought it was really no help to the play to have withdrawn it, re-cast it and re-directed it, and that if it had come in <u>at that time</u> it would probably have been a bigger success, and certainly just as good. This, to my mind is true, except that the script was just a little worse before, is better now, but should have been better still. The result – four weeks of moderate business in the Royal Court. But <u>could</u> it have been made a transfer-possibility? Who can say?!

Ayckbourn became a member of the Victoria Theatre company, Stoke-on-Trent, which staged his play Mr Whatnot *in November 1963.*

30 October 1963

Dear Peter [*Cheeseman, Director of the Victoria Theatre*],

I have now read MR. WHATNOT and I must say it's a quite stunning exercise in mime, the most unusual I have ever read. Its only problem is whether it can be done on a proscenium stage in London or whether one would simply have to use some place like LAMDA. I think this is a triumph for your theatre because I simply don't believe that Ayckbourn could have written this play without the training he has received at the Victoria.

It seems to me that everything will work except the last line. It's essential that we shouldn't see Mint until Amanda sees him but how do you get Mint on to the bed without the audience seeing him?

Please send me a list of the days when you are performing this play, plus times as I will try and come up either with Michael [*Codron*] or Peter [*Bridge*], though I should imagine a play of this sort might scare them to death and be beyond their reading powers.

Ever yours,

Ramsay was concerned where and how Mr Whatnot *might transfer to London, and was not keen to sell the option to Bridge. Ayckbourn felt loyalty to Bridge, and the play had its London premiere – Ayckbourn's first – under Bridge's management at the New Arts Theatre on 6 August 1964. It received terrible reviews and closed three weeks later.*

7 August 1964

Dear Alan,

I must also tell you that Dorothy Mather of Film Rights phoned me to say she thought it would be a brilliant idea to offer your play to Marcel Marceau!!

I told her that I think it would be a quite mad idea since Marceau writes all his own material and is a very great artist at it. In addition, the whole British background would be a perfect enigma to him.

However, I feel that I ought to tell you about her interest, and tell you frankly that I can't possibly follow this macabre suggestion. At the same time you may think she is a brilliant agent and that this idea is quite splendid. If you do, I shall entirely understand and would be perfectly prepared for you to move over to Film Rights and let them launch your career via Marceau.

I want you to be able to be perfectly free about any agent at any time, and if you think I'm too tough and not nearly enthusiastic about ideas of this sort you MUST tell me frankly and we will remain friends but you can go your own way.

I do hope you're not very depressed; believe me every talented person in the theatre has these shattering experiences either at the beginning or the middle or the end of his career. You must just learn to ride this kind of thing.

Notwithstanding all this, a great number of people enjoyed the play very much last night.

Warm wishes,

As ever,

Dear Alan,

I'm typing this myself with a heavy cold, so both hands and head will probably let me down!

I'm so glad you feel encouraged by this idiotic Peter Bridge affair – he is, as you know, totally talentless, and I tried to warn you. I don't in the least feel you to be "unmanageable", and indeed want to cheer you up and encourage you. My only concern is that you don't too often <u>caricature</u> human beings rather than <u>characterise</u> them. i.e. do strip cartoons rather than pictures! I'd love you to do a few sketches for the new Michael White-Eleanor Fazan revue – jot anything down and I'll arrange for you to meet her for a talk. I'd also like you to think about writing a comedy for television. Are you interested in writing for TV? I'd imagine you could write a good play for that medium.

If you want to come and have a talk <u>any time</u>, just phone and make a date. I'm always pleased to see you and am very anxious to start you on something else.

I must go and have a good blow!

Love,

Ayckbourn's next play, Meet My Father, *opened in Scarborough in 1965 and Bridge optioned it for London.*

Dear Peter Bridge,

What you think is "rudeness to a Manager" is my attempt to speak the truth to somebody whom I have known ever since I started as an agent. The alternative is hypocrisy – much practised in the theatre, when everyone is lying to one another face to face, but oh boy, are they tearing each other's reputations to pieces behind their backs.

A play agent has got to fight for authors, because they only have me to protect them and their families and their futures. Both of us care very much about the British theatre, so why should one pretend and not face a person and tell them the truth, when one is bitterly upset about some injustice one thinks is being done?

When you say I "make persistent attacks upon you", I am sure you are right, because I make persistent attacks upon all the London Managers. I told Peter Hall I would personally shoot the Director of his choice if he allowed him to direct one of our most outstanding plays, and he was rightly furious. Manslaughter would have been a mild price to pay for the destruction of an author, and I was perfectly serious. Recently I outraged Michael Codron by demanding that he should let me buy back a play which I felt he was destroying, and I recently accused Binkie [*Beaumont*] of dishonesty because he wanted me to give him a play which belonged to somebody else.

Maybe the true answer is that I am a very bad agent, since I have to wage these wars against Managers. Perhaps lies to their faces and innuendoes behind their backs would be another method but I think it would be contemptible.

Now we come to Alan Ayckbourn: indeed you recommended him to me with STANDING ROOM ONLY, and the fact that he had already approached me (due to the good offices of [*Peter*] Cheeseman [*Director of the Victoria Theatre*]) doesn't invalidate the fact that you wished to do me a good turn, for which I am grateful. But this doesn't mean that you have bought my loyalty to the author, and you would be the first person to agree that you weren't trying to bribe me. You were, in fact, being extremely kind.

No, I am not aware of the "great many facts about Alan and his plays" which you mention in your letter, because you have never discussed them with me, and in order that Alan should live until his play was launched, I got him a job in the BBC, Leeds, so I never see him. I only know that he has written nothing since he wrote his last play, and that he won't write anything further until this one has been done. Hence, my misery and frustration and my desire for Alan to earn enough by this play to be free to work on his next which would, of course, be offered to you.

Sincerely yours,

Meet My Father, *re-written as* Relatively Speaking, *had a pre-London try-out tour starting in Newcastle in February 1967.*

6 February 1967

My dear Alan,

I wrote another letter to Bridge, but I think I forgot to send you a copy. He was very affronted, but I was trying to tell the truth. This is, I know, a great shock to people of this sort in the Boulevard Theatre, because they always flatter each other to their faces, and say appalling things behind their backs.

We are seriously cluttered over plays. We have got Mortimer's THE JUDGE which is subject to re-writes, etc. and Bob Bolt's new play which is also subject to re-writes etc. Both are going to the provinces prior to London, like yours.

I have the feeling that Nigel Patrick [*the director*] will be absolutely in control, and would very deeply resent any comment. However, I see by my diary that I could rush up to Newcastle on the 21st, and I think I must do so. I will arrange a ticket myself at the theatre, because I don't want to sit with anybody as I want a completely uncluttered view of the play. I will let you know my hotel, and I will go heavily laden with scripts, and after the show will do some work. However, if you are going to be in a melee with the Management and director after the show, perhaps you could have breakfast with me at my hotel the following morning before I catch the train back.

Please give Michael Hordern my warmest wishes. I am glad you have Celia Johnson for your play, she was in Bob Bolt's first play and brought him heaps of luck.

I do so much hope that you are going to have a success. I even wish it for Peter Bridge in spite of our clashes, because this is a new play by a new author which is what he should be doing.

In great haste,

ever yours,

28 February 1967

My dear Alan,

Yes, I think Peter is the kindest person in the theatre manager-wise (as they say). But there's something so pre-war about it, that it's curious but positively endearing. For one thing he includes all the understudies and certain big Managers don't include stage management OR understudies in parties – a disgusting distinction.

All he needs is more taste, more perception, more judgment, and to believe that authors are just as important as stars – much much more of course, but if he can put them on the same plateau it will do to start with.

On Friday evening I sold LOOT film rights for £100,000!!! The awful thing is that I damned nearly went down to Brighton (to see the Mortimer play) by an earlier train but quite by chance I was in the office at 5.45 and clinched the deal there and then, and a cheque was rushed round to my flat just as I was off to catch the 8 p.m. train. We are now dealing with the problems of SISTER GEORGE. Bette Davis wants to buy the film rights and I think this is a way of making a mucky film. If Miss Davis is employed she might be kept in order, but if she owns the property herself!!!!…

Joe Orton has sent me his short "erotic" piece for Tynan. I don't quite know the line drawn between pornography, smut and erotic material!!!!!. Joe's is certainly indecent, but IS it erotic?????? (it's not the same at all, is it?)

I must dash. I hope you can make sense of this note. I never learned to type and now it's far too late. However it's preferable to receiving a letter in my own handwriting which is quite impossible.

Relatively Speaking opened in London in March 1967 and became Ayckbourn's first success. It proved a turning point in his career.

Dear Peter [*Bridge*],

If you are losing £1,000 a week obviously Alan will help. What seems so strange is that a play should still be running while it is losing £1,000.

Honestly it is impossible to blame the weather over the loss of revenue in a theatre. There has been nothing wrong with our weather, and many of the plays in London are doing well. I speak frankly because it is so damnably depressing to think that one has given you a play which has made you a lot of money, and which you have run to the extent that it is now losing money, and everybody has to give up royalties. None of us want you to run a play beyond the public's demand. If this were the case every single play would lose every single penny, and the theatre would be a laughing stock.

I remember that when I first started in the theatre Peter Daubeny lost an immense amount of his backing on three plays which could have succeeded, but which he ran on much too high a budget and kept on while he was losing many hundreds a week. Within a year he had lost all his backing and backers. This is appallingly bad for the theatre, not just for the Managements.

Our whole livelihood depends upon how Managements run plays, and the fact that the Duke of York's doesn't want to be dark is neither here nor there, surely? You are not a charitable institution running a play in order to oblige a West End theatre. You are one of our leading Managers, and if you don't make money there will soon be no West End Managements at all, because nobody will want to back them.

We have often had our plays quickly removed by Michael Codron, and in many respects this is preferable to an author knowing that the Management is losing an awful lot of money at the box office and he is having to take cut after cut.

We wanted you to make a great deal of money on RELATIVELY SPEAKING, and now it seems that everybody is going to talk about the play as if it were a failure. I think this is very very sad.

Warmest regards,

as ever,

3 February 1970

Dear Alan,

I don't know what you mean about "more distinguished, more so-called 'socially committed writers'" "giving permission to have their plays done in South Africa. Unless you consider Frank Marcus more "socially committed" and "distinguished" there is not one of our authors other than Marcus who agrees to South Africa, and I think it's appalling that Pieter Toerien [*producer*] should, at this stage, try and twist your arm. Were there some play which said something strong about conscience or men's relationships to one another then there might be some reason for the play to go on, but Mr. Toerien wants to put your play on to make money and entertain the whites, nothing else.

Now at a time when everybody is standing together defying South Africa to continue, you suddenly think it a good idea to let your play go on, because important authors (whoever they may be) agree to go on in South Africa. Who are these important authors? Arthur Miller doesn't agree, and he is a man who does speak for the social conscience. Even Neil Simon doesn't agree, and I would think that you and Neil Simon share something in common, because you both write high comedy, which is exceedingly popular in the theatre.

It is absolutely nothing to do with me to tell you what you should or should not do, Alan. However, I can assure you that the man who is opening the new theatre in Cape Town is going to see that in the very near future his theatre will play to both blacks and whites, and to this end they have even engaged a coloured choreographer for the ballet. You will find that in a few years' time the battle will have been won, so it seems rather silly to backslide now, merely because Peter Bridge is organising a meeting between you and Toerien.

South Africa has always lied about the number of plays that go on there. Someone like Mr. Toerien returned to South Africa announcing that he had 45 West End Plays for South Africa. They certainly never appeared there, because I don't suppose there were 45 successful West End Plays at that time. I know [*Terence*] Frisby gives permission, but Frisby is the man who spent a year in Italy rather than pay British taxes, so he is 100% for Frisby and to hell with the rest of the world. Among the authors of ours who stand firm are: John Mortimer (and South Africa, I have no doubt, would love his new plays): Peter Nichols: Robert Bolt; James Saunders, John Bowen and Alan Plater – you have already mentioned Henry Livings and David Mercer.

I think Pieter Toerien ought to spend some of his energies putting his own country right, and not so much time trying to persuade authors to have their plays seen by a select minority. Do you realise that millions of people will not be allowed to see your play, because they happen to be "inferior" from the distinguished parochial gang, who are are taking all the riches from South Africa, and making the rest of the people slaves.

Love,

Following a tour of Me Times Me *that closed in October 1971 without a London transfer, Ayckbourn and Ramsay tried to revive the play's fortunes with a tour produced by Michael Codron.*

24 November 1971

Dear Alan,

Regarding directors, I'm throwing down:

Michael Blakemore.

Peter Wood (his invention with "Jean Brodie" quite something, his help to Joe [*Orton*] over text – excellent)

Peter Hall – why not for chic!

Bob Kidd (PHILANTHROPIST good).

Robin Phillips – might be very good indeed.

These are off the top of my head, and I'm sending a copy of these suggestions to Michael [*Codron*].

Love,

PS. I don't understand [*director*] Ron Eyre's comments on murder. It is a basic part of family life, and from the moment I began dictating this postscript we have come across specific cases, including those at first hand. For instance, I tried to murder my mother by throwing a hot iron at her, and when I think about the incident I still feel the same rage and dissatisfaction at not having done it. My father knew these intermittent impulses of mine, but took them as casually as your character EDWARD. Jennie's sister [*Edward's daughter*] tried to murder her brother with a gun. She was not subsequently abandoned by her family. We could go on ad infinitum but just thought we'd make a small comment. Clearly Ron Eyre has had a very protected family life, whereas you haven't Alan! Jennie is telling us a fascinating incident about herself, but we had better leave that for a further instalment.

PPS. After reading the December Plays and Players, page 15, I think we'd better withdraw Robin Phillips' name from the list. He has made a great deal of money from ABELARD AND HELOISE, but among the terrible things he says about the play is the following extract:

"When I first read ABELARD I thought that the way we should do it so that the Woman's Own dialogue would actually be right, was to use puppets, have an Abelard and Heloise but surround them by rather large puppets so that all the sentimental chat would be theatrically valid".

He goes on to make the most appalling series of comments on a play he accepted and for which he was paid the earth.

[undated, 11 July 1972]

My dear Alan,

I don't think you should be too disappointed by Michael's reaction to the play [Time and Time Again], in toto – for instance he thought Act 2 <u>stunning</u>. In that he is quite right. I think he didn't much care for Act 1….for my part I kept seeing those two young actors in How the Other Half in that act one but it certainly didn't disconcert me. I liked them because they were so discernibly Ayckbourn characters, and I think it's essential that an author should be <u>recognised</u>, because it is his personality, and nobody else could quite write those two people.

I hope you aren't disappointed or disconcerted in my interest in your "development" of characters – I know you can do all the rest as only you can, and if, in addition, there can be a bit of fleshing, it would be pretty marvellous. And I don't mean fully drawn neurotic people sitting talking about themselves with nothing at all happening on the stage. What I really want so much is for you to be fully estimated. A really successful author is often underestimated critically – the prizes tend to go to the boys who write characters and can't write a plot if it killed them. I know you would say that Feydeau didn't write characters, but I think we can say that he was an extraordinary genius, both in his devices and in his body of work. When you write your hundredth play, I'll concede you his equal.

Nobody in the theatre can do what you do, Alan, but it would be fun if you could write character, effortlessly, as well as every OTHER author – and you can, you know, and you are demonstrating it.

I hope Tom Courtenay [*Leonard in* Time and Time Again] isn't being too cute– he needs to play against this side of his character. The pixies must remain strictly in the garden.

God, I'm off to the first night of *I, Claudius* [*stage version by Ramsay client John Mortimer*], and Tony [*Richardson, the director*] is giving a party on that Yacht which is a restaurant moored at Charing X. Do I underdress with a bikini? Perhaps we shall all get very drunk and push [*Robert*] Graves into the Thames. Tony has spent all the Capital. He has actually begun asking for cuts NOW. Oh, these fucking monsters, these geniuses of the cinema…..

11 August 1972

Dear Peter [*Bridge*],

Alan is developing away from the genre in which he wrote RELATIVELY SPEAKING and HOW THE OTHER HALF LOVES. Both of these are star vehicles, and he is no longer writing for stars of the calibre who draw the public and leave him as a successful West End author without the true praise he should be receiving.

As you know, Alan never liked the production of HOW THE OTHER HALF LOVES and with all this enormous success he has not had artistic satisfaction from it. When you say in your letter, "As it happens, Eddie [*Kulukundis*] has invited me to join him in Scarborough next Wednesday with a view to presenting this play [Absurd Person Singular] in the same manner" that is exactly what could happen, but can't happen if Michael [*Codron*] is to present the play.

The choice of a Manager must be made absolutely ruthlessly. I wouldn't feel as happy if you and Eddie were buying this new play as I feel happy about Michael doing so. This is because Michael has been entrusted with at least half a dozen of our new writers and has handled them with consummate tact and delicacy as well as efficiency.

To go back over the same old ground, you certainly presented Alan's first two plays and brought his great success and in return he brought you great success and a great deal of money and I would say that you have each benefitted from one another, but he doesn't have to have his hands tied for life if he wants to use another Manager for certain plays he writes. Eddie came into HOW THE OTHER HALF LOVES because I rang you up asking you to use him, and he has benefitted accordingly.

Both Alan and I like you very much and in certain things you are excellent. We just feel that Michael Codron would be better for this kind of play.

I feel quite unrepentant in supporting Alan, because this is the best thing for these last two plays. Quite a lot of us do a great deal for another person but the whole effort of doing a great deal is vitiated if one is demanding of the person one has helped that they can't move without one, making them a kind of slave, and a slave who has to repay the initial help for the rest of his artistic life.

Love,

Ayckbourn, who separated from his first wife, Christine, in 1971, enjoyed a long-term relationship with Heather Stoney that eventually led to marriage in 1997.

1 August 1973

Dear Heather and Alan,

I enclose a few booklets, but this is to keep you quiet!

I spoke to Stirlings Books next door, run by Mrs. Jones, whose husband is a travel agent. He is at the moment making enquiries for you. I said you would require a double cabin and must be back around December 15 to 20 and the cruise was for a month.

Cod [*Codron*] suggests the Ile de France (French Line) – a super boat – if it was going anywhere special and Mrs. Jones is finding out. We will post all details to you, and he could fix anything for you if he comes up with anything special. It seems it's very easy if you first fly to Jamaica and then cruise on (Mrs. Jones has done this) but I said you didn't want to fly <u>at all</u>, you were tired and I didn't see how one arranged one's luggage for a cruise if one flew first!

I'll be back with suggestions.

Love,

11 April 1975

Dear Alan,

I know you will enjoy and must look forward to your Windsor lunch. David Lean went fairly recently (Buck House) with a girlfriend and said she was absolutely charming, and had taken the trouble to see all his films.

Unfortunately, Wendy Hiller was there and had just played Queen Mary in CROWN MATRIMONIAL. When the Queen said that her grandmother hated using the telephone, Wendy Hiller said "Oh, no, Ma'am. In Act 11, I phoned half a dozen times." She spent the rest of the lunch contradicting all that was said about Queen Mary, saying that she had made a point of studying everything about her. David said that it was very exasperating but also very funny. Isn't it typical of an actress?

Love,

Dear Alan,

I think I've met Mr. Manim [*a South African manager*] a year or two ago at the opening, I think, of a commercial theatre. He's absolutely wrong in saying I'm fanatically anti-apartheid as an agent because this isn't true. I'm anti-apartheid as a person because I've lived in Africa, and I know what the whites are like there, and I know how the blacks are treated.

As to whether or not The Company is a good idea or not, I don't know. The real hub of the matter is the psychological effect of your giving them your play. They will make enormous capital of it, and it will look as if you approve of apartheid, which you don't.

What the authors have done is make cultural people feel ashamed. They are not depriving anyone of ideas because they can buy books and plays to read, and they can go to the cinema, though the South African Government bans anything that could possibly have any comment on the South African situation. They've just banned Rudkin's play, Ashes, which was at The Place in Cape Town because it is a very liberal play.

Peter Nichols released one of his plays, and every single newspaper in South Africa ran this as a victory for South Africa, and a defeat for the English playwrights concerned.

I don't think that HOW THE OTHER HALF LOVES is going to further the cause of liberating the blacks, or making the whites feel deeply ashamed of keeping the preponderance of the African inhabitants in bondage. (They have been offered a number of plays which have been indirectly critical of their behaviour, but those are the plays that are banned.) I think you are in the unique position of being a man who could make a lot of money from them, but who is also concerned about apartheid because of the human factor.

Moira Lister, who was a South African girl, Moira Lipshits, goes with all those comedies put on by Ray Cooney, who makes a fortune in South Africa, and I wouldn't really like you to join their club.

Oddly, we have always given permission to Rhodesia and Kenya to do plays, but they have allowed blacks in the audience, and have black actors in the theatre. But while the Pass laws prevail so that no black man can travel in South Africa without showing his Pass, or get a job without showing his Pass, and when once he has gone to jail never gets his Pass back, I don't think we should allow white South Africans to make more money for themselves out of British plays by concerned writers.

I don't think we'll have to wait very long. The ban on sport, which is the only thing that really interests South Africa, has made them realise that the way they live isn't acceptable to the humane world.

Alan, it's absolutely up to you. You can tell Mr. Manim that I don't impose my feelings on any author, though my own feelings are strongly in favour of black people being treated with the dignity that they deserve, and that they should be allowed to earn their lives according to their talents. This superior master race imposed by the white Dutch South Africans is akin to fascism. I should hate your reputation to be misjudged by what the public in South Africa is capable of. We know Ray Cooney doesn't care where one gets his money from, and that Moira Lister has to change her name in order to be acceptable to South Africa, who have been persecuting the Jews long before Hitler took on the practice. I know Moira Lister's family, so I'm not talking through my hat. I also know of the persecution of the Jews in South Africa who, of course, tend to make a lot of money, so that they can buy theatre seats the blacks can't afford, and are not welcome.

Love,

19 September 1979

My dear Alan,

I hear you open on the Friday at the end of September, but I want to come on the Monday, when the agitation has subsided – and please, please, Heather, can I have an appointment with that wonderful man round the corner from the hotel, if he can take me some time from the middle of the afternoon onwards – tell him I've been floating about on a cloud since I went to him, and I think Alan should write a play about a chiropodist!

How lovely to be reading a play of yours again [Taking Steps], it seems a long time, and I'm glad it's what you call a farce. I wonder whether the public ever look to see whether a play is called a play, or a comedy, or a farce? Plays are all doing fearfully badly in London, and managers are going grey. You're lucky not to have one on at the moment, apart from the National.

Love,

ENID BAGNOLD

*

Bagnold (1889–1981) was a distinguished novelist and playwright when on the death of her agent in 1967 she joined Ramsay. A decade before, Ramsay had written to Hugh 'Binkie' Beaumont, the most powerful manger in British theatre, with an idea for her.

13 November 1957

Dear Mr [*Hugh 'Binkie'*] Beaumont,

I know you presented THE CHALK GARDEN and I wondered if Miss Bagnold was looking for inspiration for another play. Yesterday I was invited to a small lunch at the French Embassy, and my imagination was immensely struck by Madame Chauvel the Ambassador's wife, and her husband, and an aged General, their close friend and advisor.

Madame Chauvel as you know is a rather hard middle-age [*sic*] and could never have been more than handsome, but behind that facade I kept getting glimpses of the woman. One is first struck by her patience, if one can so describe her repose.

When I arrived I asked M. Chauvel about the charabancs outside the Soviet Embassy next door, and he replied with the utmost contempt "Oh there are always charabancs outside next door – they constantly entertain teams of discus throwers or football teams" then added "I look at the Russians from my window and they all look pale, flabby and humourless (as he spoke he looked pale flabby and humourless)."

At lunch I asked her about her two girls and she said "This life is no good for the young" and she said that they had both escaped by marriage into ordinary lives.

When we were having coffee she came and offered me a cigarette and held the lighter as if her whole life was given to such gestures. Then she came and sat down by me and we began talking and she said apropos of something "I was born in South America a child of diplomats" – and I saw this long vista of her life. She then said "I used to be bad at remembering faces, but now I no longer recognise anybody" and I realised that this was an unconscious attempt to repudiate her life.

We were joined by the elderly General, whose right arm was missing and who wore the rosette in his buttonhole. He was really old, fragile and full of sensibility; he had been with them for a long time and in many countries. When he lit her cigarette (she smoked all the time, even between courses) it seemed to me that his slightly shaking hand held the lighter with special tenderness and solicitude, and when her large poodle OSCAR came and leant against my knee, he became specially friendly towards me, because her dog had shown me friendship. Suddenly I thought of the possible relationship between two such people. I wondered how young they had both been when they first met, and what it would have been if two such people had at one time loved one another, and remained together like this when it was over.

Ever since Maugham's remarkable play CAESAR'S WIFE we have never had a play about people such as these, and when you think of the lives behind these facades, what depth of feelings could there not be? And if we knew the secret lives of the protagonists, a typical diplomatic party on the stage would be very interesting. I remembered that Miss Bagnold had written a lovely book about old people and might write just such a play. I know this world is no longer like the novels of Maurice Baring (where people actually died of love!) but either Miss Bagnold or Rattigan in his DEEP BLUE SEA vein could write an enthralling play.

Yours very sincerely,

P.S. I'm afraid I've not conveyed the mystery and moving quality of these people – that is for playwrights!

28 March 1967

Dear Bobby Lantz [*US agent*],

Of course, I know all Enid Bagnold's plays. I have a weekend house in Brighton, and often pass her house in Rottingdean. But surely she has been represented in London for years? Doesn't Binkie [*Beaumont*] always do her plays? It seems to me that unless one knows her allegiances one would not be of help to her. Also, and you must forgive me this, I really cannot write to an author offering my services to her. The author must either want to come to us or we don't look after her. We just cannot tout for work however exalted the author and however brilliant. I know this sounds arrogant, but it is the opposite of arrogance – it is a form of humility.

Kindest regards,

sincerely,

29 June 1967

Dear Enid,

I would love to see you this weekend and it's sweet of you to ask me to visit. I just must be alone if I can.

I am getting up at 5.45am each morning in order to read scripts which <u>I have</u> to read, and I am having to go to a number of dress rehearsals etc. after hours so that the weekends are the only time I can try and get away from it all. I am turning down all engagements, however delectable, because I know that I shall not be able to get through any week, if I don't.

This, you see is why I hesitated about representing you. I have so many hundreds of tiny chores which MUST be done, in addition to the really IMPORTANT chores of selling and casting and Contracts. It's not just a matter of reading things, and selling and casting them, and getting jobs for the sixty or so people who rely on me to keep them, but each of them has dozens of problems – we have two plays being rehearsed for try-outs at

Scarborough, both of which must be visited; we had the whole cast of the Peter Terson play walking out of the Jeanetta Cochrane last Saturday night. We have today had to cancel rehearsals for the Arden play rehearsing for the Fortune, because the Director was so bad that all the cast complained to me. I am trying to get the GANDHI film Contract settled, the Nichols' play finally booked for a London theatre, clinch Nichols' new film deal, tell two authors that AR [*Associated Rediffusion*] now want their plays (already written) boosted from 60 minutes to 80 minutes, get a stage Contract for LOOT checked to fly to New York tonight, and inform the author we have complained about the setting up of a Director without consultation (the author is in Tangiers). Bill Naughton's play is to be transferred from the Apollo and we haven't yet fixed the theatre. I have to write all the reports on the plays I read last night and this morning. John Mortimer wants more money than provided for in his film Contract with Twentieth Century, and so does McGrath from M.G.M. These are just some of the matters which must be coped with this afternoon before I dash off to Hampstead to see the [*James*] Kennaway play…This hardly scratches the surface of what has to be dealt with TODAY!!! The idea of meeting Lantz at any time makes me moan a little. You may "engage some staff" but I want to remain small, and there are very few people gifted for this kind of job.

Love,

Noel Willman, a leading actor and director, was a close friend of Ramsay's. He was soon to direct Bagnold's play A Matter of Gravity *in the US with Katharine Hepburn and Christopher Reeve. It opened on Broadway in February 1976 after touring.*

13 June 1975

My dear Noel,

I waited till I was really fresh to read Enid's play (so I began at 6 am) – it's pretty wonderful!

I phoned you at 7.30 – I woke Jean. I then had the madness to ring Enid (I thought you were there). I told her I'd read it. Asked if she'd known ("NO")!! Oh lord.

I didn't dare continue talking to her even to ask her how she was. I really <u>fear</u> her, and have to defend myself from her. She has such a strong personality that I feel I'd be overwhelmed and be unable to do any work. I <u>mean</u> this. With Enid it's all or nothing and I must try and look after the authors I have. She would <u>overwhelm</u> me, and I'd be like Jackie [*a character in the play*] without the levitation! Is the levitation symbolic as well? It's not absolutely clear – I was shattered by the end – choosing an ugly "practical" asylum. But I suppose one <u>should</u> be shattered as Mrs. B is so <u>strong</u> and mistress supreme of her own fate (one feels that since her husband died it was the only way to survive).

One line I thought "fine writing" (which it <u>is</u> but does this matter?), the last phrase about the billiard table. Otherwise the writing is impeccable and <u>not</u> fine writing, but <u>wisdom</u>. I'll try and get this typed up.

This is the best thing Enid has written – astonishing feat.

Love,

3 March 1976

My dear Noel,

Enid says she keeps ringing, and today she caught me while she was under the dryer. She says please can I look after the Play here.

I have told her that I am sure she signed a Contract with The William Morris Agency which also gives them the right to be her agents here. She says she doesn't even remember signing a Contract, and will I please find out where it is, and whether we can look after her!!

She also tells me she's dreadfully depressed. I told her yes, success is very depressing, and I expect it's hit you in the same way.

Much love,

18 May 1976

Dear Enid,

As you see those agents whom you trusted put into the Contract that they control world rights, and they propose to hang on to them.

I shouldn't let it worry you, and as I have nothing but contempt for the William Morris Agency it doesn't worry me. However, if we can help we certainly will.

Love,

PETER BARNES

*

Barnes (1931–2004) joined Ramsay in 1963 with mainly television and screenwriting credits to his name but eager to work in theatre. Following his success in 1968 with The Ruling Class, *the Royal Shakespeare Company became interested in him and staged* The Bewitched, *directed by Terry Hands. Ramsay attended a preview.*

3 May 1974

Dear Terry,

Never have I admired you more and never, as an agent, have I felt that your company deserve the plays and playwrights worthy of the extraordinary talent and dedication you put into the theatre.

What is lacking in THE BEWITCHED is something you can't inject – profundity, depth and intellect and if these qualities are insufficient in a play of this size, it will affect the basic approach of the critics to its stature.

It's also a matter of temperament: Peter's is both the strength and weakness of his writing. He is greatly influenced by the excesses of the Jacobeans and has their exuberances, exaggerations and violence, and he is also influenced by Laurel and Hardy, but under this compact little man is a gleeful schoolboy rubbing his hands in amusement at the innocent smut of the penis-talk; sheer naughtiness entirely lacking in sexuality or eroticism. John Whiting's temperament was dark, melancholy, gentle, poetic and sensual, and this was a help to him as a serious writer. Peter's is something of

50

a handicap to his being taken seriously on the highest level. He delights in sending up the play with songs and dances but doesn't realise that this does tend to make people take the play less seriously. Shakespeare managed this with his clowns – I am not sure how.

Forgive my jotting down these random thoughts. I want to support you in every way, and if I can show my gratitude by doing anything at any time please let me know. I think from now on neither you nor Peter should treat this play as Holy Writ.

An extraordinary evening and by the First Night it should be a superbly theatrical and satisfying one.

All best wishes,

Sincerely

P.S. However, if one compares John Hopkins' trivial, domestic, self-absorbed sights with Peter's, Peter is a great man!!

30 November 1978

Dear Peter [*Hall, Director of the National Theatre*],

I have heard that you may be doing [*Kleist's*] THE PRINCE OF HOMBURG – a play which I am absolutely mad about! If you are going to do an adaptation rather than a straight translation, do you think that Peter Barnes would be good at it? He did a brilliant adaptation of [*Wedekind's*] LULU, as you know, as well as other, darker plays. Jimmie Saunders did a very, very good adaptation of Kleist's HANS KOHLHAAS. Of course, there is no reason why you should not simply do Kleist's play translated, as you have excellent translators, but I just thought I'd mention this, because I am very thrilled to hear that the National may be doing it.

Best wishes,

JOHN BARTON

*

Ramsay represented Barton (1928–2018) as an adaptor. The future Royal Shakespeare Company director formed part of Peggy's 1950s Cambridge University network, which centred on John Holmstrom, whom she represented as a translator. It embraced Tim O'Brien (whom she represented as a designer) as well as the directors Peter Hall and Peter Wood, and a subsequent generation that included the radio director/ producer John Tydeman, along with two more clients, the television playwright Ray Jenkins and the director Richard Cottrell, whom she represented as a translator/adaptor. Jenkins and Cottrell were two of the five playwrights referred to below; the others were Hugh Brogan, Tony Houghton, and Gary O'Connor.

4 May 1959

Barton dear,

Here is a cheque for £40 – I think it would be an admirable thing for you to pay [*Edward Sutro, a patron*] £10 so that you will never again forget to invite your sponsor. Indeed, I imagined that when I first told you that Edward would guarantee £100 and gave you his address that you would have immediately written thanking him. At the time I said you should do this so that you could get a letter back confirming this, as a written guarantee. I think this is a valuable lesson to me, too, never to imagine that a theatre is going to behave sensibly, and to double up over every arrangement which remotely affects me!

I have now also learned the lesson to confirm every conversation I have with you by a following letter, and as I hope we shall have many theatrical exchanges, I'm now opening a special BARTON FILE, and moving your correspondence (sparse) now in "Correspondence" into your own private file.

I loved the two shows and think it was more than worthwhile – really terribly exciting. All five plays were worth doing, and the four original ones all most interesting. O'Connor further justified himself in doing two excellent productions.

If any of the five playwrights want any professional advice, free – they are more than welcome to ask me, and I'd be more than happy to help them in any way in my power. I think you've got a rich crop of talent – writers, directors and actors, and I hope you are proud and pleased. I must say I feel a little miserable at the idea that you might desert them. Tydeman tells me that he too is on his last year. <u>What will become of your buds</u>? ? ? ?

It was lovely to see you and many thanks for inviting me and for the nice party. DON'T OVERWORK YOURSELF and try and <u>have completely silent, idle half hours at least twice a day</u> – would you promise me that??? ? ? ? (Feet up, eyes closed, and think of Schopenhauer.)

Love from,

ROBERT BOLT

*

In early 1955, at the start of her second year as an agent, Ramsay read a play by a school teacher on the suggestion of a radio script editor friend, and was convinced that R. O. Bolt (1924–1995) could become a stage writer. He had not considered this before hearing from her and subsequently sent her several efforts, each of which she damned. Her criticism and advice spurred him on until he produced a play she was prepared to send to a manager. When John Perry at H. M. Tennent rejected The Critic and the Heart, *she turned to an old friend Toby Rowland, who had recently gone into management.*

Dear Toby,

I think it IS a little difficult to know exactly what the play says, because it says a number of things. Certainly it says what Mr P has gleaned, but the young artist says something <u>else</u>, and the woman MILLICENT is there to show that life is <u>to be lived</u>, not to be given way, and if we indulge in an orgy of self-sacrifice we end by destroying the capacity to live. The author said in a letter to me that he wanted people to go home thinking "My God, yes, we're on the edge of the chasm always; we must be more careful with one another".

But I want you to consider this play very seriously. I am <u>sure</u> that this author is going to be "something" – if you <u>knew</u> how he has grown since I first met him six months ago.

If you don't want to do the play, I think I had better give it to the Arts. By all means, if you want another opinion for yourself, get Peter Hall to read it. And if you want anything clarified, the author can do it. I would like to try and sell an option on the play, because unknown to my Directors, I gave the author £95 to write this play, so feel I ought to try and earn it back!!

Much love,

Dear Mr. Campbell Williams [*manager of the Arts Theatre*],

I spoke to you this morning regarding a play [The Critic and the Heart] about which I am really excited – a six-hander. The author is coming up to London tomorrow, and I want to suggest to him certain small changes which will make it even better, so I shan't send it to you until he has done it, because I want to be <u>certain</u> that it is a winner before you read it.

Regarding "KAMPONG MALAYA" [*which Williams had rejected*] – I do so wish that you had no "rules" about war plays – I absolutely agree with you that years of experience in the theatre teaches one certain things, but there are always the exceptions ("Journey's End", for instance, was turned down by dozens of Managers and for exactly the same reason after the last war). <u>If a play is good enough for you to want to do it, you should</u> do it. If it isn't you shouldn't! Surely you didn't say about "GODOT" – "This play will make money" – you did it because you wanted to! and because of that you have your reward. I'm not only pleading for my play, I'm pleading for every play which is good.

I have been asked to the "GODOT" party tomorrow night so I shall look forward to seeing you.

Yours sincerely,

18 January 1956

Dear Mr. [*Esmé*] Percy [*actor and director*],

I hear from Robert Bolt that his friend Martin Starkie has talked to you about his plays, and you would like to read one of them with the idea that if you like it you might produce it at "Q" [*a fringe theatre in west London*].

I have not sent either "THE LAST OF THE WINE" or "FAIR MUSIC" to you yet as I am simply not sure that these plays are good enough – in any event they aren't a patch on his new one [The Critic and the Heart] which a London Management is hoping to produce. They are both exceedingly interesting but were written for radio and don't "bloom" from a stage point of view, nor are there any big roles, which makes casting difficult.

I would of course love you to read them, but I am so anxious to get Bolt properly launched as I think he has a great future, that I don't want to make any mistakes, and a debut is so important isn't it?

I expect you know that Beattie de Leon is giving up "Q" in six weeks' time, but she has another victim ready to step into her place. (I was an unlucky candidate for six months which turned out to be a fascinating but costly lesson.)

Kind regards,

Yours sincerely

Jack Minster, an actor and director whom Ramsay had helped enter into management and for whom she had read scripts, and his business partner

E. P. Clift, for whom Ramsay also had read scripts, bought an option on The Critic and the Heart *but let it expire.*

26 July 1956

Dear Jack,

I am awfully upset about this play. I more than appreciate that being associated with Clift it is very difficult indeed to press a production of anything not strictly commercial, but I had hoped that the talent of Bolt would have been found sufficient to have been given a <u>real chance</u> of going on. Apart from Margaret Vines and Flora Robson, was any other actress or actor even offered the play? And anyway, both these actresses said they loved it and wished to do it.

Thanks very much indeed for your real recognition of the play and the author's merits, and for having taken an option, even if it leads to a dead end!

Could I have the scripts of CRITIC back when you have the time. As you realise, I desperately want to try and get the play on this Autumn, and I have no script at all.

Love and thanks,

Oxford Playhouse, led by Frank Hauser, agreed to stage The Critic and the Heart, *directed by Jack Minster.*

23 February 1957

Dear Elizabeth [*Sweeting, Playhouse manager*],

I've been looking after Bolt for nearly two years and so far I haven't earned one single penny. I do this as I deeply respect his talent. If I were to give you 1% of his play, <u>I</u> wouldn't suffer, as I get 10% "off the top" [*of Bolt's 5% gross*]. But I can't bear to do this, as I KNOW he has a fine future and needs every penny in order to survive.

I don't plead for myself – I plead for the talented person Bolt is. Why didn't you ask for 5% of Lysistrata, for instance? . . . .if you demand flesh money of Bolt!!!!

Elizabeth dear, I understand your side completely. I would NEVER grudge Oxford 1% of the gross in any other play. It concerns our responsibility to talent, and I for one feel deeply about it. The only alternative I can see is for me to give up my own 10% to Oxford and go on working free. But if you knew what a similar struggle it was for a new agent to start (just the same as your own struggle) I hope you wouldn't expect this!!!!

Will you show this letter to Frank and see what he says?

Write and say if you agree to this. Honestly Bolt doesn't know how we all jump through hoops for him. I looked at my files the other day under his name, and find they are about 5 inches thick with correspondence, pleadings etc. etc. But I don't in the least mind begging for him, and I promise I'll never do it again for ordinary established talent. Let's face it, Bolt could become one of the big playwrights, if he learns, develops, and survives. Then we shall all be pleased to have helped him. And you know that any work of his would be given to your theatre before any other.

Yours,

28 February 1957

Dear Elizabeth,

I don't know why I make such an exception of Bolt. I think it's perhaps because the whole play is about sacrifice for talent, and it touches me very closely (I wouldn't have become an agent if I hadn't felt this about talent) – so that I know I ask unreasonable things for him and expect everyone to sacrifice themselves – it's all rather absurd, I know! As for Bolt himself, he is a mixture of incredible toughness and sensitivity, and I never spare him pain of any sort, but where money can be gained for him, I feel it might be just the difference between survival and oblivion. The Arts Council will do nothing for him at all – typical. I had an awful row with Linklater [*Arts Council Deputy Drama Director*] about a year before GODOT went on – he said after he read my copy that it was absolute drivel. When the play went on and he saw it, he apologised...but I haven't much faith in the Arts Council recognising <u>real</u> talent of tomorrow – in fact only people like you and Frank can, in the theatre. I'm sorry I'm trying to make you pay for it.

By the way, Robert has written another play FLOWERING CHERRY. When Frank and you have a moment please read it. You know that I would bend over backwards to let you have this play before anyone else. Perhaps we had better wait for CRITIC, and then you can see if you like it.

I can't be quite sure whether I shall come to the first night of the Lysistrata or not, or wait till the matinee. I find that if I come and stay the night, I spend more than my commission, which isn't really businesslike!!!

Best regards to you both,

Flowering Cherry *was written as a response to one of the exercises Ramsay had set Bolt, which was 'to write a play about inarticulate people, which blows up dramatically because they are unable to talk about their predicament to each other.' Ramsay showed the play to the major West End director Frith Banbury before sending it to Oxford Playhouse or Jack Minster, who was rehearsing* The Critic and the Heart.

27 March 1957

Dear Jack,

Thank you so much for your most reasonable and kind letter. Yes I DO feel I have behaved "ruthlessly" and I don't like myself very much.

I enclose a copy of the letter which Bolt wrote me and which made me, on an impulse, send the play to Banbury, never really thinking that he would offer £200 outright, and want to do it. After that move, I was stuck.

Regarding Bolt's future – I have told Mr Banbury that I will not commit Bolt's third play to anyone, and that we owed you more than anyone else the opportunity of recouping on Bolt. One of the reasons I sent the play to Banbury is that, frankly, I don't like it nearly as much as CRITIC regarding subject-matter, and I definitely think it's off-beat – so does he. He has written to [*Ralph*] Richardson about it.

All I ask is that you won't "take it out" on Bolt...please. I did what I did genuinely because I wanted to give him peace of mind and also earn him some money.

I hope you know that I always try and put anything possible your way and in the past have, I hope, always acted as your friend. Over Bolt, I suppose I am a bit emotional – I feel that his talent comes before anything else – I have such belief in him. Would you like me to say in writing to Banbury that you, as first producer of Bolt, must have the first refusal of his next play?

4 April 1957

Dear Jack,

Please don't put me <u>entirely</u> in the wrong. I take all the blame, but I did it only after thinking that CHERRY would probably get on much quicker with Banbury, who loves off-beat plays and will stick his neck out for them.

CRITIC is a much more unusual play, but I can see myself how <u>very</u> difficult it is to cast for London. So is CHERRY, and it's much more depressing and drab.

God knows, I shall not have anybody in the world talking to me soon... but the alternative is to play the managers' game, and betray the authors. (Perhaps this is the only thing possible in the West End?)

Yours,

Flowering Cherry was taken up by H. M. Tennent, the most influential management in the country, and starred Ralph Richardson and Celia Johnson. Frith Banbury directed.

22 August 1957

Dear Mr. Banbury,

As an agent I want to be seen and heard only when I can be of use. But at the same time, I feel I know you well enough, and Bolt and I owe you so much, that I hope you will not be annoyed if I say how very depressed I am by the preliminary announcements of the play [Flowering Cherry]. Dare I tell you – strictly for what it is worth – that if I read these descriptions about another play, I would say to myself that as far as I was concerned I would give that play a miss…..

The particular point stressed in the publicity seems to be that the play is about the incompatibility of two people married <u>during the 1914/1918 war</u>. Now this to me means a play of my parents' generation, and obviously the children of such a couple would have been born about 1920, which means that they are now over early 37 apiece…. In fact two old people, with no-longer-young children unable to settle down after nearly forty years together….! If I feel like this – and I am middle-aged – what will everyone <u>under</u> forty feel?

I do hope you are not angry with my writing frankly like this and please would you allow this letter to be strictly confidential, and not shown to anybody else?

Kindest regards,

Sincerely,

23 August 1957

Dear Mr. Banbury,

Just to complete my letter of yesterday about the publicity for FLOWERING CHERRY and then I will keep silent.

Surely the play's theme is far far deeper than a mere inspection of incompatibility between husband and wife?

CHERRY seems to me to be the prototype of a million ordinary men who work for their living in the city, but who have their roots in the country. His dreams are the extension of every office worker who cultivates a small garden and this starvation and longing for "something to grow" is deep in the English character.

But CHERRY's real dilemma is that he has lost his self-respect. <u>Because of this</u> – because of his failure to succeed in his city job – his masculinity is shaken and his sex-life has gone wrong, and with it his relationship as head of the family. It is because he wants them to be proud of him that he escapes from his mediocrity into dreams, and then into lies, into "showing off" in front of one of his daughter's friends, and into petty theft.

Harold Hobson and I were talking about Richardson the other day and he was saying that he was the greatest actor in England. I said that I thought his genius lay in making the ordinary seem extraordinary, and that when Richardson plays the "average man in the street" he transforms him into something deeply moving, and mysterious, and important, and wonderful.

Surely this play depicts the contemporary predicament of the average man in a materialistic age – and the "incompatibility" with his wife is only a small part of the total human condition and the <u>outcome</u> of trying to live in a competitive world, in the barren city.

I feel I ought to try and enlarge upon my note of yesterday.

Kindest regards,

Barbara Bray was the radio drama script editor who introduced Ramsay to Bolt's writing.

9 October 1957

Dear Barbara,

Yes, indeed, I do fear that there will be comments about CHERRY and DEATH OF A SALESMAN. One worry about this is that the Miller play was so much more for your money! (Four rooms instead of one and a flower-bed, more scenes, more sex, and a juggling with time)

This play is not so depressing – no funeral – and the 'transfiguration' at the end will cheer us all up (though what it means, if anything, I DON'T know......!) Personally I think this play is just another step in the career of Robert Bolt, and I am rather alarmed that with the stars and the grand theatre and management, people will imagine that this is the peak of a career, instead of the beginning.

Yours ever,

Hugh Beaumont, managing director of H.M. Tennent, was producing Flowering Cherry.

Dear Mr. Beaumont,

Naturally I know <u>you</u> by sight, but I specially did not ask to be introduced as I saw you were looking after Lady Richardson, and I know stars' wives are dynamite – (upon what she says to him in the bedroom after the show may hang the fate of the play!). It seemed to me that I could only have murmured something banal, and that you ought to be spared!

I will not write about the first performance except to say that I was glad a lot of things did not go properly, because these mistakes and longeurs lead everybody to improve everything.

Bolt does not make it easy for actors, as it is so difficult for them to judge the boundaries, and the limitations, of their parts. And he has no technical skill in contrasting his scenes so that the most cold-blooded assessing is needed so that nothing drools or is repetitious – in the effects, in the playing, in the moves, everything. Bolt never says to himself (like Rattigan) "does this hold, does this <u>finally</u> entertain"…..

He gives a particularly awful problem with his ending, relying as he does on the scenic effect to lift the play emotionally and poetically.

I had imagined that Reece [*Pemberton, the designer*] was going to build a *kitchen* set in front of a sky cyclorama, and that this foreground set was either to be transparent, and disappear with lighting or be "flown" so that when CHERRY at last reaches his dreams, we would be free of the Kitchen altogether, and the stage would be entirely "his dream". Did you see (by any chance) the Kurfurstendam Theatre's recent production of WOZZECK? Caspar Neher, the designer, had a front-set of a typical facade of German houses, which though realistically painted, were, in substance, faintly transparent, and through this faint transparency one saw an enormous cyclorama of winter sky and at the foot of the sky, marshes. As you know, WOZZECK kills his sweetheart and finally drowns himself in the marshes, and by our seeing them in the distance, it was as if we were waiting for them, and after a time one began to long to see them, one was drawn towards them, and when we finally reached this simple expanse of sky and marsh, thought the events were tragic, it was what we had been waiting for the whole evening as if Wozzeck's death was not only inevitable, but acceptable and indeed, had a tragic beauty.

This is a very exaggerated comparison to draw, but I think in CHERRY we ought to be caught up in his dream, and that each time his dream should come nearer i.e. the lights should be intensified and the music go just a little bit further at each visitation, until at the end we get it totally, and the music completed itself (the way in a symphony the theme is intimated, is elaborated, and finally bursts out in its complete and perfect form). Am I writing nonsense? I am trying to express an emotional need in the play!

How odd it is that Sir Ralph brings all sorts of miraculous things of his own to the play while not yet being at his best in Bolt's best scenes – for instance "look at my tears" should play better than it does, and that simple speech about the country and the men under the trees and the church is meaningless at the moment because it is so elaborately "broken-up" (but perhaps this speech is anyway too literary and does not work, off the page?)

It was so sad that Dudy Nimmo had taken such a dislike to the girl "Judy" [*the role she played*] – she seemed to have "judged and condemned" her, and was commenting on her, instead of trying to <u>give her a case</u>, for, of course, she has one. There are thousands of gauche, intense, tiresome, plain young women, living in banal homes, longing for "culture" and yearning for beauty and therefore attaching themselves to a more integrated, more beautiful friend.

Perhaps if you are in Oxford on Monday night (and they can possibly squeeze me in), I will try and say "How do you do" to you, if I see you un-occupied for a second!

Meanwhile it is an immense comfort to think that Bolt's play is in your hands. I am sure he has a "future" and can only hope, for all your sakes, that he has a "present" too.

Yours sincerely,

23 October 1957

Dear Mr Beaumont,

Many thanks for your letter and the cutting. I went up to see the play last night, and I hope you won't think I am being a nuisance, or exceeding my position, if I "report".

First, I'm glad Bob Bolt is behaving well – he is supremely happy to be working close to you.

Last night no music was used, except the "poker" music and the final music. Unfortunately, torn from its context, the final music sounded pretty bad – unctuous and treacly, and of an organ texture: it made one think of those "heavenly choirs" in those Hollywood films. When one is conditioned to it from the start one doesn't notice its quality at the end! Everything else seemed much better and Mr Banbury was extremely kind in allowing a free discussion of many minor details.

The real crux of the problem is that neither set nor music are ideal. This isn't, naturally, said in any spirit of criticism – it's so easy for the outsider to say "if only"….! Reece has gone for his inspiration to the folksy plays of America – THE WOODEN DISH, SALESMAN, etc., and it's been planned in this tradition – one which anyway always tends to drabness and is now almost a cliché, but in this case it doesn't actually solve all the difficulties. As for the music, Mr Banbury, I think, is very anxious not to be thought sentimental or ham, and to avoid Palm-Court or Ketèlby [*composer known for light orchestral music*] or pseudo-Tchaikovsky he has settled for a rather watery "modern", who doesn't do any harm to the play, but doesn't actually help it sufficiently.

This isn't criticism: I know that all these things are now part of the play, and that if they are with us it is fundamentally my fault, because if I had sent you the script in the first place one thing might not have led to another. (I ran "Q" Theatre for six months where I learned that the first steps are the important ones, and irrevocable, and after that one can only do things in relation to those first steps.) Nor do I want you to think for an instant this is any criticism of Mr Banbury – of course it isn't.

Seeing the play from the circle last night, the final transformation seemed better, because we were plunged into what was clearly a dense growth of trees (not mere dappling – from the stalls the dresser and the plates dominate too much). But what we need emotionally is blossom – a drift of pale blossoms. I don't really know much about Somerset, but I lived in Japan as a child and the cherry blossom there is something I can never, never forget – it filled the universe. And CHERRY'S dream is, after all, based on childhood memories, which are stronger, more beautiful, more abundant than they ever were in reality, don't you think? I don't mean the vision should be necessarily the kind of thing Tree did at His Majesty's (live rabbits, real grass!) – it could be totally unrealistic, but it must overwhelm us emotionally; it must "come up strong" and we should be anguished when it fades and we are left with a man in a kitchen. (By the way, both "curtains" were badly mis-timed last night.)

I hope you don't mind my writing like this – the play seems to be getting better all the time.

Yours very sincerely,

Dear Frith Banbury,

I'm taking my courage in my hands (as they say) and writing to you to tell you what has been growing inside me since I saw the play at Liverpool, and though it was wonderfully improved at Oxford, it still doesn't quieten this inner voice!

It's quite baldly this: as agent for Bolt it's his career I care about, not just this one play. If I thought this play as it stood would be an artistic success and a commercial failure I would think your money well lost! But it CANNOT be an "artistic suicide" – the play is a straightforward play of emotion and relationship. The set is in the tradition of the modern American play and breaks no new ground, the music doesn't startle in its originality, it isn't as angry as Osborne, or as poetic as Fry and Tennessee Williams, or as avant-garde as Ionesco. Certainly it has the problem of being a realistic play with what seems to be unrealistic moments. But are these moments unrealistic? Nor really, CHERRY dreams, and we have decided to "illustrate" his dreams, that's all. It's a commercial success in embryo.

I began my life in the theatre with the Carl Rosa Opera Company, and we played FAUST. When the old FAUST sat in his study in Act One, he dreamed of MARGUERITE, and the gauze scenery behind him became transparent and we saw clearly MARGUERITE at her spinning-wheel. Then she faded out and we went on with the song! Nobody said that this was a "realistic" opera with "unrealistic" scenes – they were just moved to see a lovely young girl evoked by an old man, and when FAUST met this girl later in the play (after he had regained his youth in order to meet her, selling his soul in the process) it was damnably moving and what everybody in the audience wanted – they wanted to be young, to meet the "girl of the dreams" etc. It was the most popular opera in the repertoire.

Isn't CHERRY the same problem? He dreams, we see his dream, and we must want it.

Now, to the next point. It's that of feeling. I'm going to digress over this and I hope you won't mind. Here is what De Maupassant says on the subject of his writing: "We must FEEL, that is everything. We must feel as a brute beast feels, and knows that it has felt, and knows that each feeling shakes like an earthquake".

Here is what Quiller-Couch says about great literature: "Is it possible that you can have read one, two or three of the acknowledged masterpieces of literature without having it borne on you that they are great because they are alive and traffic not with celestial certainties, but with men's hopes, aspirations, doubts, loves, hates, breakups of the heart; the glory and vanity of human endeavour, the transience of beauty, the capricious uncertain lease on which you and I hold life, the dark coast to which we inevitably steer; all that amuses or vexes, all that sadden, gladden, maddens us in men and women on this brief and mutable traject which yet must be home for a while…."

Tennessee Williams says: "because we do not participate we can view the people on the stage with the limitations of our emotional equipment. They do not return our looks, we do not have to answer their questions nor make any sign of being in company with them – for this reason we are able to see them; or hearts are wrung by recognition and pity."

I don't think that anybody loses face or is an object of ridicule because he accepts feeling, provided it is true feeling and not sentimentality. Is Marlowe "ham" because he writes something as theatrical as:

> Why this is Hell, nor am I out of it:
> Think thou that I who saw the face of God
> And tasted the eternal joys of heaven
> Am not tormented with ten thousand hells

In being deprived of everlasting bliss?

Nor is Baudelaire to be despised because he writes frankly on the highest possible emotional revealment

"Je te donne ces vers afin que si mon nom

Aborde heureusement aux epoques lointaines

Et fait rever un soir les cervelles humaines…

Ta memoire paraille aux fables incertaines

Fatigue le lecteur ainsi qu'un tympanon…"

could anything be more grandiose and ham?

And here is what Havelock Ellis, the philosopher, writes about his wife:

"Whenever nowadays I go up to London, I come upon places where we met: here she stood: here we sat together: just as even in places where she never went I come upon some object, however trifling, which leads me by a thread of suggestion, to her. So that sometimes it seems to me that at every step of my feet and at every movement of my thoughts I see before me something which speaks of her, and my heart grows suddenly tender and my lips move involuntarily 'my darling'."

This, from a man of reason and an "intellectual."

And what about Ovid?

Dum licet, et vernos etiamnum educitis annos

(While you can and are still in your spring flower, have your sport)

Ludite: eunt anni more fluentis aquae

(for the years pass like flowing water)

Nec quae praeteriit, iterum revocabitur unda

(the wave that has gone cannot be called back)

Ne quae praeteriit, hora redire potest…

(the hour that has gone cannot return.)…

I translate because the Latin is probably inaccurate.

I could go on for pages, but will finish with two Gide quotations: here is the first, when he was fifty, and in love with a youth:

"Immense delirium of happiness – my joy has something untamed, wild, incompatible with all decency, all propriety, all law. Through it I return to the stammering of my childhood, for it offers my mind nothing but novelty. I need to convert everything, words and gestures; nothing of the past satisfies my love any longer. Everything in me blossoms forth; is amazed; my heart beats wildly an excess of life rises to my throat like a sob. I no longer know anything......."

(Isn't this magnificent? This man doesn't fear ridicule, he speaks the full truth and revels in that truth. How can one not love him?)

Here is Gide again, saying what should be found in every play:

..."you will come when I have ceased to hear the noises of this earth and to taste its dews upon my lips – perhaps you are not sufficiently amazed at being alive; you do not wonder as you should at this astounding miracle of your life, I sometimes feel that it is with my thirst that you will drink, and that what inclines you to that other creature you caress, is my own desire"......

As I've started quoting, I may as well finish the letter on the same lines! Here is something from D.H. Lawrence which is the kind of thing we should feel about CHERRY:

"With man it is always Spring – or it may be; with him every day is a blossoming day, if he will. He is a plant eternally in flower, he is an animal eternally in rut, he is a bird eternally in song."

And "Phèdre" is one scene after another of pure feeling – with the anguish screwed to the furthest point possible, like an orgasm. Lorca's poetry is pure feeling (not intellect), so is Verlaine, so is Thomas Wyatt, so is Ronsard, and Villon:

Prince, n'enquerez de sepmaine

Ou elles sont, ne de cest an,

Qu'a ce refrain ne vous remaine

Mais ou sont les neiges d'antan....

and Heine, yes, and Propertius, Pirandello....

Can you forgive this outpouring? I'm simply pleading for the maximum amount of feeling to be drawn out of the play, and every possible weapon used in order to allow the characters to reach out to us over the footlights, telling us that we are not alone in the world; that other human beings live, suffer and play the fool.

Next time I'll try and write a proper letter,

Warmest regards,

P.S. My God, this is appallingly typed, and I don't know whether the letter conveys at all what I am trying to say!

Flowering Cherry *was a hit when it opened in the West End, and Bolt's subsequent successes on stage and in film transformed both his fortunes and the fortunes of Ramsay's agency. Beaumont presented Bolt's* The Tiger and the Horse *and* A Man for All Seasons, *directed by Noel Willman, and then wanted a new play from Bolt, who in the meantime had been hired by producer Sam Spiegel to work on the film script of* Lawrence of Arabia.

5 June 1961

Dear Binkie,

I know you would like to know the position regarding Bob and the Lawrence film, so confidentially I am sending you the letter I've just written Spiegel with our terms. If he will accept – and he told me I could make our own contract – then Bob could "stay" with the film (and win an <u>Oscar</u>) and yet devote all the time he wishes to his play.

I know both you and Noel would like a complete break [*from the film*], but this subject (Lawrence) is so magnificent, and the "rushes" make us believe that it's real Oscar stuff, so that if we could win Bob a high esteem in the film world, and then reject the films in future, it will help his prestige, and there is no doubt at all that he has learned some quite remarkable things by working on this project. He has, I hasten to say, no intention of doing another film in the foreseeable future, and I doubt if in a decade another subject of this sort will present itself. So please try and understand.

I think both Noel and you feel that I am, perhaps, a little too lenient with my clients and don't sufficiently keep them "in order". I must tell you now that I deliberately refrain from "dictating" because, in fact, at no stage has it been so serious that intervention on my part was necessary.

It seems to me one should refrain from using pressure until it becomes a serious necessity, then, by virtue of one's previous moderation, one has every chance of being listened to. (If this sounds a bit Madame Machiavelli, well, there it is!)

Kindest regards,

4 December 1963

Dear Bob,

Once an author has become successful and famous, it becomes more difficult to speak the truth, and this is why people like Rattigan become bloodless, because, in time, people fear to give them anything but lip service for self-preservation's sake.

Love,

Lawrence of Arabia *was a triumph but the new play for Beaumont,* Gentle Jack, *was not.*

20 January 1964

My dear Bob,

So – from Rome to Spain. For god's sake remember the Corruption of the Grand Hotels (which you happen to hate, and which I love, having been dragged from one Grand Hotel to another through Europe when my parents were travelling round and round the world).

I'm rather pleased today, because I received a fascinating new script from a young man [*Joe Orton*] on Jan 1, met the author a few days later, sold the play to Michael Codron and Donald Albery this morning and it goes on in March. And Chatto and Windus will publish. I suppose he is the answer to Pinter (NOT Bolt) but his influence is Firbank and Genet, instead of Beckett. The author has just come out of Wormwood Scrubs, for thieving and bodily violence, but I'd trust my life to him or any of my possessions. He is 25.

You are lucky to be away. The theatre generally is moribund. Binkie wants to let GENTLE JACK continue and he has been marvellous throughout.

For some reason I feel in splendid heart about you. I want us to have a long long talk about all the things which concern me at the moment. You pick up these things so remarkably and transmute them to something important.

My dear boy, life is really a very exciting and tremendous thing. We ought to celebrate this fact more often. I think it's right, too, that you should have had an experience of failure. The thing is to have experienced everything before the last great experience which waits for us all.

Love,

31 January 1964

My dear Bob,

The new, young jail-bird playwright is, I imagine, an interesting minor talent, certainly not a major talent at least not yet discernibly so. Peter Wood will do his little play [Entertaining Mr Sloane] and I think we may get Terence Stamp but it will only be done at the Arts. I'm just touched by a young creature who had this odd experience and has come out so simple and pure. He has a very attractive personality and I'm thankful that I read his play first and met him afterwards.

Alan Schneider and I had drinks with Beckett last night. Alan says Pinter has become hideously spoilt and silly – Beckett, of course, the opposite. I'm going to the first night of VIRGINIA WOOLF and tomorrow night am going to The Theatre of Cruelty – a complete waste of time, I'm sure. I went to Paris last week-end and saw five plays and was dazzled by the French acting talent. Seeing [*Frisch's*] ANDORRA, I thought Tom Courtenay perfectly ridiculous – no range, no technique and very little of anything else. The production rather slow and ponderous but the message of the play certainly came home to me in no uncertain terms, though it won't be a success.

It's rather nice to be quite alone in the flat and I'm feeling very calm and co-ordinated you will be pleased to hear.

Much love,

When Peter Hall founded the Royal Shakespeare Company in 1960, he offered Bolt a commission, which he declined, preferring to remain for the time with Binkie Beaumont and the commercial sector. Not wishing to give up, Hall discussed with Beaumont a co-production of a Bolt play about Elizabeth I and Mary Queen of Scots (at one point called Remarkable Women, *later to become* Vivat! Vivat Regina!*). Negotiations dragged on but led nowhere and the play eventually was produced at Chichester.*

5 February 1964

My dear Bob,

I lunched with [*Peter*] Hall. It's terrifying to watch the effect of his maniacal will to power, which is almost destroying him. My God, why doesn't he read Schopenhauer and see the danger he is in. The slightest opposition, and he is like Hitler, screaming. When I said "You <u>ought</u> to have bought that play" he nearly had apoplexy. A distinct folie-de-grandeur which is alarming to see, because it's so dangerous and because it's now "built in" and nobody can warn him. He will brook <u>no opposition</u>. He wants to be loved, but my God, I <u>can't</u> love him. When he claimed that your play was "his" he meant to say that his discussion with you was directly reflected in your play. I can believe it. But he doesn't like the play, you know. Anyway, all he says about it boils down to the fact that he wants you to write for him and to submit entirely to him and his will.

Binkie is a far, far better man, with all his limitations, because loyalty is the keystone to his character, and love for people, absurd people, who gossip and love and slip up and so forth. Utterly "human". Hall isn't human, and one glimpses the bodies of the victims whom he has destroyed on his climb up to power. I think he is actually in danger – either his health will crack altogether or he might have a kind of seizure. For God's sake, keep this letter <u>utterly</u> confidential.

By the way, when you write your next play, don't discuss it with Hall, if you can restrain yourself. I don't think he is a good person to be with during the gestation period. I mean this seriously. But after saying all this, I deeply admire what he has done – but at <u>what a price</u>. It has left him a broken man, thirsting for submission. He and I will <u>never</u> hit it off, though it is my tiny bit of opposition which is to blame. I have just one per cent of what drives Hall and this he can't take and hates. He spots it and loathes it, because he knows he is <u>entirely</u> compounded of it.

Love,

11 August 1964

My dear Bob,

I saw the new Sybil Thorndike vehicle at Brighton last night [Season of Goodwill] – honestly, it's pathetic. By Arthur Marshall and it would be a fair disgrace in 1920. It might run in town for a few months because both Thorndike and [Gwen] Ffrangcon-Davies have marathons, and dull people who don't want to think might sit through it. The press is bound to be bad for the play, because it's not a proper play at all. There ARE no plays!!!

I don't quite know how we can all <u>control</u> our lives, and not let work eat them all up, do you? As long as we are absorbing and learning, it's O.K, but to be a mere pack-horse for money is <u>absurd</u>. The trouble is that to live a proper full life one needs the modicum of food and decent dwelling and travelling is almost a <u>must</u> – but to work 50 weeks of the year for this isn't quite sane. You are working to pay rent, rates, taxes, agent, accountant and lawyer, and feed and clothe your young. You must see to it that you earn only just sufficient for this purpose, <u>not more</u>! We can all live more simply, and give ourselves time to think and feel and see. We don't need better cars, more clothes, bric-a-brac or luxuries – just enough to enjoy and fulfil ourselves. All these town houses, mammoth offices, fleets of secretaries, business lunches – <u>ludicrous</u>.

The sun is shining and it's rather pleasant outside.

Love,

17 August 1964

My dear Bob,

I can't quite say why I felt so sad to receive your letter about accepting the nomination for Governorship of the Royal Shakespeare.

As you know, my one desire is to <u>serve</u> talent, and my only interest is <u>in that talent</u>, its emergence, and its development. With this development come the rewards – "success" (the killer). The development at the same time of an author's aspirations towards power and manipulation of his chosen field. All this is fulfilling oneself as a human being in a particular community, (the rebel becoming the established figure, etc. etc...).

What really worries me is this "development", and the effect it has on the original creative talent. My sadness extends not only to you, but (perhaps impertinently) to Peter too. This man Hall had a marvellous creative talent, he was way ahead of everyone, he did remarkable things because of the necessities of his talent to create. We now have a great powerful figure, one of the few to emerge at the top of the tree – but we have lost the remarkable, selfless creative human being – the person who operated alone, and who changed our theatre by his single talent.

Then there is the "image" which time inexorably builds – yours is getting a bit "set", and though the image doesn't truly represent the man, I'm dead scared of your ending up a committee man, a lecture man, a Director man, and like J. B. Priestley end up a boring, preaching <u>dead</u> man, who is all weight and nothing much else. Under Priestley's weight is a struggling eager <u>young</u> man, entirely buried in all the tasks he has undertaken, all the responsibilities he has taken on, all the honours which have been handed to him. So – he had twenty years of creativity, and over twenty of this weighty important gentleman who will be "Priestley" until he dies, and then the creative man will re-assert himself, because he won't be there boring <u>us</u> to death.

Love,

My dear Bob,

I'm typing this at mad speed myself.

Yes, I've seen [*Roy*] Rosetti [*second unit director,* Doctor Zhivago] – I'm giving him my first night seats for the Osborne play [Inadmissible Evidence]. I have been lumbered with seats next to all the Press, as I think they feel I might want to help with a judicious word. I don't. I've seen a rehearsal and this long monologue isn't well done either by Nicol [*Williamson*] or Anthony Page [*the director*], and it doesn't really come off, though the lighting, set, first night excitement might well drive it over the footlights. I think Osborne and the Court should stand on their own feet, and I want to keep all my energies for my clients who need it even more than Osborne does…. hope you don't think this is selfish. I gave away the seats almost instinctively, and now I'm trying to justify why I'm not going myself…

Now: re Peter Hall. Binkie told me that Hall had told him six months ago that he was "going to steal him from Binkie and that the next Bolt play would belong to Hall". Binkie phoned me at the time and I had no comment to make, but said that certainly you and Hall were very good friends and that you were thinking of a children's play for the Aldwych. Binkie will think that this Stratford offer is a direct bribe, but I don't believe this to be the case – I think you'd be simply splendid, but that at the present time it was absolutely essential for you to write two or three stage plays, and that nothing in the world should stand in your way.

I saw the new Graham Greene play [Father Carving a Statue] at Brighton. Perhaps it's [*Ralph*] Richardson who is the reminder but the Greene play is somehow like a very inept, very bad CHERRY, but full of cosmic references (God the Father, the Son; God the indifferent etc., etc.). Binkie is terribly worried because it is <u>obscure</u>. The awful part is that I suppose it IS difficult to know what Greene is actually <u>about</u>, but I don't really care. I found the play largely uninteresting, except for its echoes of CHERRY (he even lifted a heavy iron bar!). A very grand set, beautifully lit. But the artist in the play is so <u>old fashioned</u> – the whole play seems to me to be heavy and older than I am (which is saying something), and I for one am not in the least interested in trying to clarify why Greene is saying. I'm just <u>indifferent</u>. I suppose the play may run until the Spring and it may get very respectful treatment.

But take it from me, it's a play to <u>skip</u>. In a way the Osborne play needed Richardson, and the two plays rolled into one would have been just that much better and made one tolerable evening.

Bob: let nothing stop you from writing for the next couple of years, please. NOW IS THE TIME. Don't allow Binkie, Hall or any other "interested party" snatch you from <u>your own task</u>, which is to write a good play. I'm bored with all these people with their bribes and grabs and self-seeking. You have to defend yourself or you'll be eaten alive by them. They are, in their way, as bad as Spiegel.

This note probably doesn't make sense. I've been reading plays till I'm dropping. And today Noel [*Willman*] has flown the Vidal and the Wheeler from New York telling me to read them immediately and report fully at once. In addition we have six plays in rehearsal, all opening out of London next week – absurd!

Love,

5 October 1964

My dear Bob,

We already HAVE this pro-rata deal incorporated in your existing Contract [*for* Doctor Zhivago], and for god's sake, you have given them (as you say) at least 10 weeks beyond the time laid out in this Contract, so OF COURSE we must get you pro-rata, in order to give you freedom. A lump sum offer above what you have already received (I mean what you WILL have received when they settle the final payment when you deliver) would mean that they will be able to have first demand on your time until the whole film is finished which means too that all next year will be spent at the heels of David Lean [Doctor Zhivago *director*]. A THOUSAND TIMES NO. Other writers do a script and are left off the hook – why not you? You aren't being <u>paid</u> to produce, or cast, or being even offered a profit-royalty. Why should you even consider this matter? It seems to me that David Lean is dominating you by these months under the same roof, and the sooner you are under your own the better.

YOU DO NOT WANT TO BE ON CALL. If they want you for extra weeks' work, they must pay you and (if necessary) you must have the right to say your own work prevents your presence. Unless we are totally firm, you will find yourself sucked into this enterprise. I am prepared to be an absolute dragon on your behalf and fight to the death for your freedom.

Now: about when you start writing your play. I beg you, really beg you, to go into this as if you are about to dedicate yourself to some religious festival! The word in the Bolt household must be <u>SACRIFICE</u> – and this goes for you, Jo [*Bolt's ex-wife*] and the kids.

It's difficult to know exactly what I mean about sacrifice – I think I mean that you shouldn't allow yourself any of the indulgences that success and money have brought. NO "living it up", no escapes to grand hotels, no "special benefits"….I am very serious about this. You must live exactly as your audience lives, with all the concerns which we have all the time. I am certain that this is essential if you are to write a play which is to strike us bang in the middle. I often think that the only reason I am doing well (financially) as an agent, is because I live the same way as the very ordinary man in the street, and therefore am totally in touch with his desires, fears and so forth. I have no special privileges of any sort, and I have no "escape". Quite unconsciously both you and Jo use the escape route of privilege, and did so during the writing of the last play.

I hope you won't think it impertinent of me to <u>beg</u> you to sacrifice all luxuries and all treats. Make 1965 an extended Lent. Ask everyone in the family to observe this – they will be surprised how exciting and stimulating this discipline will be. They are all beginning to get a little out of touch –

I know it's almost impossible to be "normal" with Lean within cable reach and Sam [*Spiegel*] within telephone communication, but <u>it must be done</u>. Try and let it be as it was while you were writing MAN. If you cheat on this, your play will be less good, I promise you. I feel it absolutely in my bones.

Much love,

Bolt was set to work on a film adaptation of Madame Bovary *for David Lean, which later became* Ryan's Daughter.

4 October 1966

My dear Bob,

When you next play a record of – say – Bartók, see if you could "simplify" his work by saying he wished to "entertain". And do please read the letters which illuminate BOVARY before you start writing BOVARY. I'm sure you have a copy of the selection in English (only a small selection by the way). If not, please let me give them to you.

As for Shakespeare – my conjecture was that he wrote to the fullest extent of his talent, and that he wrote <u>for himself</u>, while earning his living at the same time: the perfect combination. Perhaps a genius <u>can</u> simply celebrate his talent – if Mozart did "entertain" it's because he was always driven by money and had one of the purest most perfect gifts possible. But, you know I don't believe that jugglers merely want to "entertain" – they seek a kind of perfection <u>in their craft</u> for its own sake, which only other jugglers can understand. It would be quite easy to be a so-so juggler and "entertain" since we (the public) don't understand which tricks are easy and which are difficult and vice versa. I have also seen "entertaining" jugglers, who "sell out" to their audience.

Certainly Emile Littler, Binkie or Mike Frankovitch are satisfied with this word, but I think you are underestimating your audience (in exactly the same way the New York Managers underestimate their audiences, by "emptying" their plays of content to make them just "entertaining"), and if you think the audiences come <u>merely</u> to be entertained, <u>you are wrong</u>.

First, look at your audiences today – they are uncertain about their jobs, full of bitterness and queries. Do they want to escape into "entertainment" or do they want to try and find help and sustenance – even though the sustenance is buried deep in the play – not just "said" (as entertainments "say" something, on the surface).

My own problem is to try and prepare myself to behave well when infirmity, illness and death come. "Entertainment" isn't likely to help me on this, but a great number of plays do – Shakespeare's for instance.

Liszt is the supreme entertainer – a working pianist, who embroidered like mad and exhibited himself for the pleasure of gushing and excited empty-headed ladies. If Liszt had restrained himself, he might have left something worthy. Obviously he could have been an "artist" if all that applause and fame and money hadn't gone to his head, but he became a mere entertainer.

One works for oneself – explores all the talents one has and tried to perfect them by technical means – if the result is entertainment well and good, but it's irrelevant.

When you jeer at the new writers you are jeering because they haven't yet learned the technique, which they are all trying to grasp. You stress what they CAN'T do, not honour what they CAN. But if one runs away with the idea that a well turned play, full of technical accomplishment, is the answer, I don't think it is, in these difficult times. One's goal should be secret, a determination to explore the human animal and to understand it. Not necessarily "psychologically", sometimes mysteriously in symbols, like the avant-garde, sometimes straightforward – it's all the same.

Nobody should be pompous and grand about their work – I don't think that work should actually be discussed – I mean the intention of the writer, or artist or musician.

I don't believe for one moment that this is how you write, and I can only suppose that working with film people has given you a vocabulary which is inadequate in discussing your work.

Much love,

P.S. I am afraid Noel [*Willman*] would entirely agree with your statement and absolutely refute mine. He hates everything new, it seems. ON the other hand he is tremendously intelligent and cultivated – perhaps he is right and I'M unrepentantly wrong!

<u>CONFIDENTIAL</u>

Dear Sir Laurence [*Olivier, Director of the National Theatre*],

I hope you will forgive me for bothering you personally about a contract with your theatre which is still unsigned. I feel that only you can decide whether or not the negotiations between the National and Robert Bolt for [*Ibsen's*] THE PRETENDERS could be withdrawn.

The problem is, in short, that Bob Bolt has asked me if I could make this request. I have told him that I will do my best, but I feel that a rather full explanation is the only way I can excuse our asking for this.

Yesterday Bob returned from Hollywood (where he went for the Oscar ceremony) and he and I had a very serious talk. I have felt for some time that Bob is only intermittently giving his full attention to writing. He has always felt that he is foremost a family man and secondly a writer. Even since the disaster of his marriage, he still feels that his children come before his work, and puts all work on one side if they visit him.

I know that everyone must choose the attitude he takes towards his work, and if he puts his life first and his work second this is perfectly alright, if the resulting work is sufficiently good. Unfortunately, the recent film script Bob has written (not yet shown to anyone but myself), and the play now on tour, cannot be considered the best he is capable of doing.

When two of his most recent pieces of work are, to my mind, substandard, obviously it is my job as his agent to say so, loud and clear. As soon as Bob arrived off the plane, I had a very serious talk to him, and explained to him that unless he was to be a dedicated writer, rather than a merely professional writer, then he would quite soon become a hack. (I don't have to explain to you what I mean by a "dedicated" person towards their job because you afford the perfect example of such a person.)

Bob has now to entirely rewrite BROTHER AND SISTER [*a reworking of* The Critic and the Heart], and during our discussion he knows what must be done – and <u>it is radical</u>. The play is on tour and must come to the Brighton Festival virtually as it stands and the tour continues for a further two weeks after Brighton. Bob can make certain peripheral improvements for the tour, but this play, as it stands, must not come to London. Bob must rewrite and it will take at least two months. He must also rewrite his screenplay, which will take another three months.

It may be that nobody will want to do the new version of BROTHER AND SISTER after the present version is seen and criticised. But even if it should never be done, he <u>must</u> write the play he should have written. He must also entirely rewrite the screenplay. From now on, above all, he must be <u>continuously</u> a writer, not sometimes a writer and sometimes a man. He will find that the better writer he is, the better the man (monster though he might become!)

If he is to do the work on the two things he has ill-done, he can't take on THE PRETENDERS during this year. Will you release him? It would make a great deal of difference to his career and character if he were made to discipline himself in this way, and I promise you that one day he will repay you artistically for this defection.

I hope very much that you won't mind my having written the full truth. It is always so much better than prevarications and lies. Perhaps you would let me know if you are prepared to allow us to leave the contract unsigned.

Kind regards,

Sincerely,

Bolt agreed to cancel a production of Brother and Sister, *directed by Frith Banbury, during its pre-London tour.*

1 May 1967

Dear Frith,

It really was splendid of you to write that enthusiastic and concerned letter about BROTHER AND SISTER.

In your letter you say that "everyone concerned should summon up <u>a bit of courage</u> and at least go down with flags flying".

Surely to decide to pull the play out and start all over again is even more courageous? I don't see why it's brave to go down with flags flying. Is it brave to risk doing something which both the Management and author think could be done better?

When I first became an agent Margery Vosper said to me that a play was like a racehorse and that its chances of success were similar to a punter sticking a pin into a list of runners.

I so disagree with this assessment. I think that survival depends upon talent, and part of talent is to criticise one's own work not love it because it owns one. Nor do I honestly think that because a production exists that it should come in "in its own right". If this came in and failed, it would be bad for Bob and just as bad for Binkie. Binkie has faith in Bob, and thinks that if he is determined to do major re-writes, then he should be given the opportunity to be able to do them. Neither Bob nor Binkie are afraid of failure, they just don't think the play is as good as it <u>could</u> be. I do agree that it is utterly wretched for the cast, who are innocently involved in all this and whose fault it is not.

LOOT was withdrawn after a long tour, which one could say was a production "in its own right". But difficult as it was to withdraw, the results of the re-production have entirely altered the career of the author for the better, though Kenneth Williams paid some of the bill.

As you said about this version, who can tell whether it would have succeeded or not, and who can predict what a new version might do? We can only wait until Bob has written the new play and Binkie has done it. So let's talk again in, say, two years' time, and then we shall know whether it was a good idea or a bad idea. I stand on the side-lines with passionate interest and concern.

Ever yours,

Ramsay wanted a new production of Brother and Sister, *which Bolt was re-writing.*

15 September 1967

Dear Bob,

Regarding Directing: I'm still a bit unsure whether you will get the best out of the play without the tension of another person asking you questions. I feel it's terribly important for us to get a really super production and make no mistakes. I feel very concerned about you at the present time, and feel somehow that we are making something of a mess of your career. It's not going at all the way I would wish it to go (I can't speak for you).

My feeling is that you are still at the beginning of a very big career with many new plays and films still to be written, yet our attitude (and yours) is rather as if you're the grand old man who can do whatever he wishes. I don't think this is true at all. I think we need to work and fight for your career, as never before. The couple of Oscars [*for* Doctor Zhivago *and* A Man for All Seasons] are not in the least helpful: I spit on them. I want us to struggle as if from square one.

I am voicing my real true feeling about your career. I shan't hide my worries, because I want to spur you to take this business incredibly seriously. I feel sometimes as if I'm trying to talk to some kind of sybarite who has eluded me. Why do I feel this? It's not just puritanism, it's based on some area of fact!!!!!!! Of course I'd really like you back to no running water and the lavatory a bog at the end of the garden. No, I don't wish this, but I'm always aware that a career can turn full circle, and Norman Hunter, for instance, is indeed back in some tiny cottage in some tiny village and I turned down his last two plays.

So, Bob let's pull the collars of our overcoats up over our ears, and let's pull our hats over our heads and grimly GO FORWARD. If we don't do this, we might go back.

Love,

17 June 1969

Dear Bob,

We will talk long and hard about your directing your own play. I keep telling you to direct someone else's – to try it out on the dog as it were. If you direct your own play nothing will be added to it. I also have feverish memories of the horror of the designer you chose for THE TIGER AND THE HORSE and the design you wanted imposed on A MAN FOR ALL SEASONS. In fact, I worry about your visual talent vis a vis the theatre. I also think you have a hideous repressed passion for acting. I remember, for instance, your not allowing me to read GENTLE JACK, but ordering me to come to you on Sunday afternoon where I had to sit for three or four hours listening to a recording of your performing every single part. In this way I wasn't able to judge the play properly, because I had no idea what it was like when it was performed by one actor. There was also the time when you nearly lost Paul Scofield, because you wanted to read him the part. This hideous and very suspect exhibitionist side of your nature should be allowed to come out, the way pus should be removed from a wound, but is your play the best way of getting rid of all this.

There is just a tiny bit of truth in the last outrageous sentence. I do think you long to perform in a lot of ways and you have never had a chance since you stopped haranguing little boys as a schoolmaster. You have never had a chance to act or direct so that these things are still buried inside you.

As for our managing the play, I don't think we can talk about this until we see if the play is very good. If this is the best thing you have ever written, I think it might be a very good idea. I imagine the only way to be the Management with Binkie is for us to form a small production company, or use Amethyst Productions (which are our own) and put up half the money, while at the same time demanding artistic control.

So, let's keep all this in abeyance until the play is finished. I don't want us to mess it up Bob, if it's very good. A number of actors might turn it down if they think the author is going to breathe down their necks, and the play might have a better chance if you have a "pure" Director. At the moment, no "pure" Director springs to mind, though we could get a young man called Richard Eyre for instance who would co-direct with you, but he isn't going to command marvellous actors. On the other hand, we don't want a typical H.M. Tennent cast, because this no longer works. Joe Orton's last play was fusty with that clutter of old fashioned Actors, and dreary old fashioned Director, and that bloody awful Hutchinson Scott set.

Binkie has even buggered up Feydeau [Cat Among the Pigeons, *adapted by John Mortimer*]. We have been on cuts since the first performance. If he can't pull off his own kind of thing, how is he going to pull off something else?

Why shouldn't you enjoy writing this play? I don't think marvellous things only come from anguish – I mean anguish at the actual time of execution, I think things come because one had anguish beforehand, and you have had plenty – quite enough to carry you through the next six plays.

Love,

Bolt and his second wife, the actor Sarah Miles, were in rehearsal for his play Vivat! Vivat Regina!

5 May 1970

Dear Bob,

I feel I must write to you about my concern for the condition I found both you and Sarah in. I know you have had to work continuously this year, but you have simply got to begin to build a store of inner calm and peace, and above all build some kind of inner life, which is inviolable.

Ever since I have known you I have found a tremendous storm tossed family, and I think all these continuous crises were responsible for the break-up of your marriage. Unless you and Sarah can absolutely put calm and peace as a priority in your lives you are going to hurt one another personally and hurt both your careers. Maybe you will have to do a course of yoga or go to a hypnotist or take a course in relaxation, but please start the moment this letter arrives. There are still three weeks of rehearsal, and when Sarah isn't rehearsing she must absolutely cultivate peace at any price.

You are both very successful and you both have plenty of money. You also have a happy home and a marvellous little boy. Count your blessings Bob, and all you have to do is to try and retain whatever you have and if you live in the affirmative you will do this. Throw out all feelings of fear and competition, and most of all this applies to Sarah. She must take time off to think about Mary Queen of Scots as a person, and feel that she is being allowed to tell her story – there should be a kind of inner communication between these people, and you should get a kind of touching pleasure in going through the chosen situation of her life. This should be a quiet link between her and the woman who lived many years ago – a kind of stretching out between the generations.

I don't remember feeling more concerned about you both, but I know you will take this letter seriously and really try hard to remove turmoil and stress from your lives. Start every morning afresh, enjoy every step of it, do your work and then dismiss it, and snatch some peace and quiet whenever you can.

Love to you both,

Bolt was in Bora Bora, Polynesia. His play State of the Revolution *had been nominated for Play of the Year in the Society of West End Theatre awards.*

8 December 1977

Dear Bob,

The West End managers gave Henry de Montherlant's 50-year-old play [The Fire that Consumes] the prize, thus ruffling few feathers. Montherlant, of course, is dead, perhaps the best thing for a playwright to win prizes.

Love,

Bolt was in Tahiti working on a film script of Mutiny on the Bounty *for David Lean and had complained to Ramsay about the financial arrangements.*

18 July 1978 [handwritten]

Dear Bob,

If I hadn't heard from you personally, I'd have suggested we said "goodbye", and thanked you for your endless loyalty to me. If you'd like to go – you should do so, as you owe me nothing – I owe you far more for the years I've been associated with your extraordinary artistic development.

BUT the pressure of the life and the hard people – the <u>unartistic</u> ones – is bound to blunt one. It has blunted us all. But it's more <u>serious</u> for a writer of your calibre and I care a great deal that the burden you have been carrying for years isn't paid for by blunting of sensibilities. Talent CAN harden and that is the only thing I care about. Luckily I don't have large families and responsibilities, only a tiny firm [?], and I'm not bludgeoned the same way. This probably makes me react too superficially and <u>not</u> take into account the appalling, continuous pressure upon you.

Believe me, you haven't changed but there's the danger of a carapace of a kind of <u>lime</u>-like substance, like a hardened tap where the hard water leaves its deposit – in a kettle! This in the end prevents the kettle and tap from functioning properly.

You don't <u>know</u>, quite, how <u>all</u> these problems and efforts are dangerous to you ... and few people will tell you, as few people remember you poor and unknown. They fear to "offend" you. I may be clumsy but I <u>do</u> want to tell the truth to YOU –

I see this toll success exacts and to the lesser writers they are back again where they started. A minor writer, but relatively successful, Frederick Raphael, is back contributing to a TV serial on <u>Rothschild</u>, where he started! Peter Nichols has just written a 6-part TV on his career which is full of hate and malice, and I've <u>tried</u> to tell him that without love and compassion an author is <u>nothing</u>.

Love as ever,

Bolt stayed with Ramsay. After he suffered a stroke in 1979, he was re-united with Sarah Miles; they had divorced in 1976. She looked after him until his death in 1995.

22 November 1984

My dear Sarah,

I am absolutely at a loss to understand your letter – why on earth would I be suspicious of you? Bob wouldn't be with you if he didn't want to be, and I think it is very brave of a young girl to live her life with somebody who will never be fit again.

All that ever made me wince was when you were at the height of your exhibitionism, but you are not so now, you are thoughtful and kind.

I don't understand why everybody thinks only about themselves, there is a chip on one's shoulder if people think everybody else is criticising them. There is absolutely nothing for me to criticise or be suspicious about. For God's sake, what about? There are too many other important things to think about to feel suspicious about people, and I am only delighted that you and Bob are together again and I think that Bob is extremely lucky. Could we stop thinking about suspicion? I am very pleased to think about you but I don't spend my time brooding about you. There are other people who need help and a great deal of thought. You are an extremely pretty girl and there is a great deal in life for you to live for, so please stop thinking about yourself. I would have thought that India would have taught you to look outwards not inwards.

Let's not behave like this – your letter took me by surprise, if you don't feel like talking, why shouldn't you not talk?

Love,

EDWARD BOND

*

On the strength of his first play, The Pope's Wedding, *which the Royal Court presented in 1962 as a Sunday evening production without décor, the theatre commissioned a new play from Bond (1934–), who had no agent. Ramsay received enquiries about the new play,* Saved, *because it was assumed, given her association with playwrights staged by the Royal Court, she was Bond's agent.* Saved *opened in November 1965.*

Dear Mr. Bond,

I feel rather uncomfortable, as an agent writing to an author who has sold a play himself to a theatre, and has no agent.

We have been asked by several of our foreign agents about your play [Saved], and for this reason we rang up the Court to ask who represented you so that we could give this information to our foreign colleagues. They told me you have not an agent.

We could do either of two things, pass on to you any enquiry we get so that you can answer and deal with things yourself, or we could ask alternatively whether you would allow us to read your play and then come to you suggesting that we might represent you in areas which you require, provided we honestly feel that we could be of real service to you and offer you sufficient enthusiasm.

It would be nice to find an author who just doesn't want an agent – I believe Donleavy is such a man, and you may well be another Donleavy. I am personally torn between thinking agents parasites, and thinking the work they do is worth very much more than the 10% they demand. You may have very firm ideas on this subject!

Anyway we leave it to you to answer this letter any way you wish, or not answer it at all.

Very good wishes for your play.

Sincerely yours,

6 October 1965

Dear Edward Bond,

Good heavens, I am not comparing your writing to Donleavy's, he came to mind because his is one of the few writers who cocks a snoot at agents, and one can't help liking him for it!

I have not read your play, so I can't possibly whore after your talent (which is, oddly enough the one interesting thing in being an agent.). I hear the play is very violent. I do hope the audience isn't going to behave as if it is attending a public hanging. I remember at the first night at Stratford East when they played the Behan play [The Quare Fellow], I happened to be sitting in the first row of the circle and looked round at the faces hanging over the balustrade and they were all grinning like lunatics – getting a kick <u>out of</u> the hanging. Well it certainly isn't such a long time since Tyburn, and we certainly haven't changed our natures. I greatly look forward to seeing what <u>kind</u> of play you have written and what effect you want it to have, and what effect it actually has. An author has this marvellous power to communicate to people – a sort of secret which isn't in the words of the plot. I do envy you this power.

Good wishes,

yours,

Bond joined Ramsay and remained with her until her death.

14 August 1969

Dear Edward,

We were talking about Diaghilev, and indeed anyone who lives by the talent of others, you forget that the impetus and raison d'être is <u>for</u> talent, but the appalling detailed work which goes to get something like a ballet on the stage, or even an author "served", is infinitely, infinitely <u>boring</u>. The outsiders think how marvellous it was for Diaghilev to have been surrounded by geniuses, but without all the boring work which is never considered, known or discussed, these geniuses wouldn't have painted, written or danced. His main headache was the interminable hunt for money, since his metier was too expensive to pay for itself. In the more humble reaches of agencies, the good ones seldom last, or stick it, because <u>in itself</u> it required the almost impossible from anyone who decides to do this job.

First, there is the essential recognition of talent; this means recognising something which nobody else has yet recognised, not a mere matter of reading a very good author's play and saying it's excellent – a thousand people can do that, and they usually declare a play to be very good because of perhaps its faults – "fine writing", i.e. literary talent has nothing to do with dramatic talent. (It's a matter of originality, selection and choice and timing, only then the theme hidden behind everything, the dynamic propulsion forward, etc. etc. etc.) Having spotted original unknown talent there is then the task of assessing the author's character in one or two brief meetings. Not just his potential writing talent, but his character <u>now</u>, as an unknown, and his character <u>as it will be</u> – under the stress of failure, and the even greater stress of success. Every author is entirely <u>different</u> – you cannot imagine the difference between the talents; all of them almost unique, if they are strong. We usually meet an author as a bachelor, but what, for God's sake, is he going to be like when he sets up home with someone else? (Look at the effect of Margaretta on John Arden; his writing, his thinking, his being. Nobody could have predicted John's development, say ten years ago, and accurately guessed what he has become today – I mean for good as well as for bad, like the rest of us!)

Then there's the whole of the world of the creatures who inhabit the "market" – each one with a different lack of talent, each one an individual who must be a channel for the products of the author or painter or musician. And the "media" are entirely different. Anyone who thinks that writing for the stage is in any way similar to TV, or that writing for TV has anything to do with films, is mad, and incapable of judgement. In the case of all these media, in any case, it's not just a matter of what is possible NOW, but what <u>could</u> and might be possible in the future. Which brings me to the business of constantly renewing yourself, constantly being able to develop, yet stay in the same job, with the same people, in the same building. If one doesn't renew inside one suddenly stops: like Binkie, who MADE the British actors-theatre in the '30s and '40s, but too late began to try and catch up when he found that this theatre no longer existed. (But it is now coming back, not because anyone wants it, but because, for some reason the people who launched the '60s, have taken a sabbatical, without knowing it.)

So the talent is an infinite and continuous pleasure, the pleasures – one of many – <u>inside the head</u>. But what of the rest? An agent needs diabolical powers of negotiating and manipulating and persuading – shady and tricky talents to develop, since all the while they must not become a pleasure or a true talent, but merely something which has to be used, with honour, for a legitimate purpose. As soon as it becomes a pleasure, he is <u>corrupted</u>. During struggle most of the temptations are hidden – to work is to live – I mean eat and just pay the rent – so this is a safe primitive drive for survival. But when the rent is paid, when there is a little money in the bank, when the agent has met a lot of people – what then? Pleasure beckons, but must be resisted; friendships must be curtailed (since friendship takes up time, dissipates the antennae of recognition), late nights make it impossible to work during the day. As for love – nobody still capable of catching that disease DARE fall potently in love as dozens of lives depend on someone who is reasonably sane! So we come back to the supreme example of Diaghilev, the head of everything in this talent-line. If he hadn't loved Nijinsky, if he hadn't loved Lifar – and I mean obsessive love (and creatures who deal in talent must by their very nature be obsessive) Nijinsky would still perhaps have been alive, and the Russian Ballet of Diaghilev's would certainly not have foundered (the war was a matter of five years and he could have picked up the reins afterwards but for this disease, you know).

So, the first ten years are easy – if anyone survives and still recognises talent for ten years – but then some kind of wisdom accumulates, and the creature who is still struggling to launch talent begins to read people without their saying anything, begins to know what is going to happen before it happens, begins to find that as soon as a play in manuscript arrives, let's say, that they can predict, <u>while reading</u>, not just the virtue of the play, but the whole history of the play – the casting, the production, the critics' reactions, its destiny, in fact. All this comes instantaneously, like a creation of a short story. The details vary a little, but the whole picture is hideously accurate. So it takes all the weary steps, and the going through of what <u>is already known</u> has to be lived through.

Where are the great impresarios nowadays? [*Harold*] Fielding, Rudolf Bing? Bernard Delfont? You're joking. They are money-makers, despoiling and exploiting talent. George [*Devine*]'s role is divided between <u>Directors</u>, not impresarios.

As for agents, where are they? The big offices merely sell "goods". Gareth [*Wigan*] had real talent, a small genius for figures and deals, and intimations of talent and goodness. He left – a success – utterly bored and horrified, and one was delighted when he escaped. One of the woman agents in London lives because she drinks to get her through the day. One or two have goodish

92

assistants, but the assistants are writing books, translating, doing anything rather than do the same work over and over again.

It's this dual requirement which is so burdensome. A really good, equipped, business talent, can find its mark in thousands of fields. There are millions of good businessmen, good Managers, good accountants, good assistants, good managing directors. And not a few good perceptive people who recognise talent – at once I think of [*John*] Calder and Michael White. But we both know that Calder has none of the business acumen or stability and that White is forced to make more and more money, and puts on OH! CALCUTTA!, instead of certain things he knows about, but can't afford to do.

I suppose it's like everything else. It's <u>character</u> which makes for survival, the capability of struggling towards independence, and THEN THE ability to stay as humble as when you started, the resistance to pomposity, and superiority and conventionality and selfishness and resistance to jealousy of the creative, greed, or miserliness, or fear of the future (so that everything is geared to what will happen at 60, whereas nobody at all can ensure the world and its inexorable events, and we are just pawns of these events when they come, and to sacrifice one's life for safety at 70 is the most pathetic thing of all). So – everyone who dares play with talent, without having the actual talent, or developing their own has these weaknesses.

All the things I list as weaknesses and failures I have myself. And added to it, a kind of wildness, due, I think to having been brought up in countries with wide landscapes, cruel colours, brutal draughts, the whole indifference of nature set before my eyes. It's like expecting a wild cat to live in a suburban house and not claw the furniture and tear up the curtains!

Love from,

[undated, September 1971; handwritten, after seeing Bond's Lear]
Edward – What can I say? A terrifying, terrible experience, but as you said, full of healing pity and understanding.

93

A young woman behind me was shattered. She collapsed in Act II and had to be comforted by her companion. But – to my <u>amazement</u> – returned for Act III!!

Going out, another girl said to her escort: "Edward Bond is <u>five thousand times</u> as talented as Osborne!!"

All the same – if the theatre was always like this – <u>could one survive</u>?

You are becoming a <u>great master</u>, my dear.

Love,

JOHN BOWEN

*

Bowen (1924–), a novelist who joined Ramsay in 1961 when he turned to writing for the theatre and television as well, sent her a play by his partner David Cook, which she declined to represent.

25 July 1966

Dear John,

I may be quite wrong, but I have as much right to be wrong as right, and the only thing that the authors I represent can do is to leave me, and that's alright too.

Even with our own authors I reserve the right to ask if I might not look after the play. I have just done this in the case of a very important play by Peter Nichols [A Day in the Death of Joe Egg]. I was so shocked by his depicting a child of ten having a series of fits on the stage that I didn't feel I could bring myself to show it to anybody. Of course, I risk the possibility of losing him, but I just can't look after the play. In a quite different way I can't at this time, with fairness to David Cook, look after his play. I wouldn't have been sufficiently enthusiastic about it, and therefore he wouldn't have found me as good an agent as he should have found me.

Love,

P.S. By a curious coincidence I have had a letter from Peter Nichols this morning. I do hope you will notice his extraordinary magnanimity, and his grasp of the fact that I would not be the best agent for the play, feeling as I do. I think I behaved with honour towards him. It is perfectly easy to send out a play with a covering letter, and there was nothing to stop me sending David Cook's play to the four TV companies with a charming letter, but I tried to tell you that I didn't think I was the best person. I am afraid this may be considered a virtue of this company, but it also has certain disadvantages.

29 July 1966

Dear John,

What you don't seem to grasp is the fact that agents are not any different from authors when it comes to the possibility that they may be knocked off balance. I have tried to explain to you that I couldn't focus the play, and I have tried to explain to you that I am frightfully churned up about the general situation. I know it isn't helpful to be churned up and that one ought to do something about it and pull oneself together, but unless a play has something to do with life at the moment, or is so strong, or so funny, or so crude that it can break through, I just can't keep my attention on it. It would be very nice to go away for a month's holiday, or to stop worrying about the general situation – neither is really possible in the circumstances, and I am afraid David's play came at a time when it was impossible for me to be of help. I am not saying I am right, because I keep apologising, but you really must stay your anger, because anger doesn't give me my equilibrium the way a hysterical person's equilibrium might be re-adjusted by a slap on the face. Unfortunately, my symptoms are not of hysteria, but of depression and concern for the general mess everywhere. It doesn't make one as good an agent as one should be.

Love,

My dear John,

Any woman is a mother, lover or governess and it depends upon the day of the week, the time of day, the year, the events of the night preceding the morning of the letter, etc. In the office I tend to be nothing but governess, because of the filthy pressure. However, all three are there all the time, but perhaps we can play down the mother, as I don't think this is really my metier.

I do understand your anxiety. I don't think the returns are promising. Of course it would help for the play [After the Rain] to run, but we all knew the risk of no stars in this particular play would certainly endanger the chances of the play. Therefore we haven't any right to complain. All we can do is to wait grimly and be hopeful.

Love,

Bowen's Robin Redbreast *had been broadcast on television in 1970. Ramsay was trying to interest Bernard Miles, who ran the Mermaid Theatre, in a stage version.*

17 February 1972

Dear Bernard,

I do so understand your revulsion to the Dutch cap in John's play. Anyone virile and with a strong sex life must feel this. But, the whole point of the play is vested in this damnable little contraption, because the play is against the frigidity engendered by our so called civilisation and modern way of life, versus the old primeval "natural" world of nature.

This poor bloody finicky bitch, with an obviously boring and perfunctory sex life in the city (and the BBC to boot!) finds herself with country folk who still allow the old gods to function. I think it's up to the actress to play the first part like an efficient working woman with an awkward and clumsy nature (only too exaggerated), and then this person is rescued by nature, meets Pan, and the Midsummer Night's Dream. When she mentions the cap, she finds it almost impossible to speak the word, she is so shy and inhibited. After she has had a natural lover, she blossoms into a real woman.

I do think the cause of Nature should be spoken for Bernard, and because you have always been a "natural" man, I imagine that you don't fully realise the enormous amount of people who have been crippled by pudeur and false modesty and crude sexuality.

I think this is an interesting play, celebrating Pan as it does and that it will be splendid on your stage. I hope you will realise that the Cap is being <u>attacked</u>, and all it stands for, and that we should think it a symbol of the rubberised world of today, contrasted with the nearest thing to Arcadia that we can find in this country.

Best wishes

PS: Eddie [*Kulukundis*], of course, is Greek, and therefore entirely untouched by the problem! (They manage things better in Greece!)

8 March 1972

Dear Bernard,

The whole point about the Pill is that it is an extended course of pills for someone who needs the precaution continually. Those other devices are for occasional excursions.

I think the heroine of this play would be mad to be taking pills every day, because she has no steady need for it. If girls become ill, the first thing a doctor does is to stop their pill and they move to other forms such as the dreaded 'Cap'.

Strangely enough, only the other day someone here said that they were feeling a little ill, and I said that maybe it was the Pill. She replied that she didn't use it because she had no continual need for it. I did not like to ask what she used, but perhaps I should have done so.

I wish we could find out what the 'Cap' turnover is. I have a feeling that if we knew, both you and I would change our metier.

I hope you admire the delicacy and euphemism of this letter.

Warm regards,

Yours sincerely,

Dear John,

Michael Meyer [*a Ramsay client*] reconstructed a short documentary based on the findings of Emilie Bardach's letters and journal about Ibsen, whom she met one summer when he was 60 and she was 18.

The interest in the documentary lies in Ibsen's character – a man with desires, he was inhibited from consummating. Married to a wife who must have known all about him and to whom he owed his success (he once said to her that she was his character).

He was therefore virtually a prisoner since I imagine that writing plays was the first passion of his life and without her he wouldn't have been able to do so. However, in their particular society it wasn't really possible to have love on the side. At any rate, Ibsen didn't have any love affair after his marriage – (before he married he had two affairs; one was at the age of 16 when he had a baby by a servant girl, and the next was a girl whose parents refused to allow him to marry her, because of his original affair, and they threatened to get him out of the theatre he was working in – i.e. the first time he chose playwriting before "love").

But what interested me particularly was the <u>peripheral</u> plot. When Ibsen didn't run away with Bardach (Michael Meyer does not suggest that they did more than perhaps kiss), and when he returned home, he did not keep up the very dangerous original correspondence, but elected a <u>substitute</u>. Young girl, who had been at the hotel when he met Emilie. The same dangerous flirtation – again no more (obviously as Meyer's reconstruction was from "evidence", only what actually happened is touched on).

But what <u>about</u> a play about a <u>substitute</u> love? I know Goethe had a smashing idea: that you slept with your wife but imagined it was the girl you were in love with, but I mean a scene with the <u>substitute</u> which is almost identical with the original scene and a complete substitution for the object of love. It's only part of a plot, but I don't think it's been used.

If you're interested in the idea of <u>repetition</u> the best thing about DEATH IN VENICE is when the hero observes and is horrified by an old man painted to look young in a group of young men. Later, of course, when he is obsessed by Tadzio he goes to the barber and has <u>his</u> hair dyed and his face painted.

The most interesting part of the Mann episode is, of course, the man's original horror, as if his subconscious recognised what was in store for him.

Love,

HOWARD BRENTON

*

Brenton (1942–) joined Ramsay in 1974, following his friend and co-writer David Hare, and stayed until her death.

12 February 1976

Dear Howard,

We have been asked by the National Theatre whether we would like to take a page or half a page of their commemorative programme to use for advertising.

I have replied that we never advertise and I think it would be awfully vulgar and repulsive to do so, and anyway who wants to read a commemorative programme of show-biz ads.

I have therefore suggested that we are not averse to helping the commemorative programme provided this space is used for something really meaningful. Of course they have no ideas and have left me stuck with it. I had wondered if there was some really marvellous person who could be asked to write something in the programme, which will reflect what we hope the National are aiming for, but not in terms of plugging the theatre, but I have now had another idea: do you think it might be possible for you to find the time and inclination to choose something of Neruda's, which really stood on its own and was appropriate to a commemorative programme of a season which is hoping to open its doors to several kinds of person? If you think you could suggest anything and if you are in the least bit sympathetic towards what you think I am groping towards saying, could you please give me a ring?

I have always said about Hare that the best things in his plays are the quotes at the beginning!! They are always wonderful quotes and they make the mind dizzy. What about a page or half a page of something which makes everybody's minds dizzy?

Love,

6 July 1976

My dear Howard,

When you say the National should pay an author £60 a week for a year that means they would have to pay him over £3000 a year. I am sure they could do this for about a dozen authors, but all you get at the end is a fortnight's run at the Cottesloe, and what happens to the other 99% of the authors? What about an author who comes up this year after the National have given out the subs? Playwrights are a long continuous chain and they can't all be subsidised.

This whole business of adaptors and translators worries me. When I think that Ibsen never had £1000 in his life and there are dozens of adaptors earning enormous sums through big West End productions I feel desperate, but one should not despair on Ibsen, because half of his character was built on this determination to become a marvellous writer.

I wonder what has happened to the many hundreds of writers who have received Arts Council grants. Of course the talented ones like yourself survive because of it, but I know many dozens with small talents who got grants such as yours, but who is to judge a talent before it emerges.

Actors now get a living wage but at the price of thousands of out-of-work actors. I am not arguing against support for authors or tremendously good Contracts – what I am thinking about is how a few will benefit, and how many will not.

Love,

Dear Howard,

I can't tell you how much I admire you for turning down Brandeis University. I wish other authors would avoid temptation because of their work, as two of our authors, to say the least, are absolutely behindhand because they can't resist a free jaunt, and the spotlight on themselves when they get there.

Much Love,

19 January 1983

Dear Max [*Stafford-Clark, Royal Court Artistic Director*],

I do understand how, from your point of view, you feel that the Royal Court is totally committed to the authors. From our point of view, and I speak for both myself and my clients, we don't feel the same way.

It is a very subtle feeling, that when you are setting up a play the choice of director, designer and staff is more important to you than whether the author is happy with all such people. I greatly admire your loyalty to your team, but I cannot say that we have always been happy with the results. It is not that these people are not good at their jobs, but they are not always the right people for the play. I do not go into further details.

If you like Howard's play [The Genius], and if you want to do it, it needs a more Jocelyn Herbert set, in so much as it needs, if seems to me, space; not bits of cardboard, cardboard doors and windows, and that kind of thing, because if one cannot spend a lot of money the sets often look like cardboard. (Although I do like the way you are creeping perspex into plays!).

I mention all this because I think Howard's play could be killed by the wrong designer, just as one of Edward [*Bond*]'s plays, directed by Bill [*Gaskill*], which had nothing but a bare polished floor was quite beautiful.

Before I was an Agent I ran a theatre. A mistake over the choice of director, designer, play, actors and lighting was crucial. In fact the major thing I learnt was that a play is a success or failure on the first day of rehearsal, and when one sat a dress rehearsal a mistake in one of the ingredients simply shattered one.

Your choice of authors and plays is most admirable, and I have no complaints now, although in the past when an author had to wait for over a year before a commissioned play was put on was deadly, because for 18 months an author couldn't work at anything else and became suicidal.

I think the basic problem with the theatre, particularly the Court, is that not enough money goes on to the stage itself. I remember hearing about the structure of the Royal Court, and how enormous amounts of money were absorbed by a lot of things, and therefore there is only a limited amount of money for staging the play. But no theatre will ever be entirely satisfactory until the money is put on to the stage, which is the reason for the theatre being there in the first place.

Warm regards,

Sincerely yours,

BRIGID BROPHY

*

Brophy (1929–95), a novelist and critic, had had one play, The Burglar, *produced (at The Vaudeville Theatre, directed by Frank Dunlop) when her literary agent approached Ramsay with a new play. Ramsay represented Brophy until 1971.*

26 August 1968

Dear Anne [*Graham Bell, Brophy's literary agent*],

Here is an interim report of my homework.

I took THE BURGLAR away for the weekend, as it seemed sensible to read Miss Brophy's first play before commencing her latest [Love Now, Die Later].

As I told you on the phone we have been trying to resist taking on any further playwrights, except those of such outstanding worth that it would make nonsense of being an agent if one were to refuse the chance.

I had begun with a slight prejudice against Miss Brophy – thinking that she might be too intelligent, and too "intellectual" to become a playwright. There should remain something of the child to help one communicate with a mixed body such as one finds in an average audience. I had also remembered seeing Miss Brophy "savage" somebody on TV – somebody quite unable to defend themselves. Though they richly deserved to be punished, one was, somehow, upset and distressed by the person who dished it out. (Yes, I remember who it was, a fox hunting man, who was defending his disgusting sport, and god knows I loathed him, but I also remember feeling that if I ever could have had any sympathy for him it would have been due to Miss Brophy's attack.)

I mention these trivial points, because I want to stress that I didn't begin reading the play with love and admiration for the writer. But within two pages I was full of admiration for her wit, talent and professionalism. The play is altogether an admirable example of its kind, and it seems to me to be a quite exceptional play from a not-yet-established playwright.

What it lacks, of course, is any interest in the <u>possibilities</u> of the visual theatre. I don't mean that a playwright should indulge in mere virtuosity of technique, but Miss Brophy has got a room, a window and a bed, and the Director has got to arrange endless permutations of the moves in order to interest the eye.

When the author calls the play a "farce" of course she is quite right, but much of Feydeau's success is due to the "va et vient" of the characters, in and out of doors, sliding down staircases, and so forth. Feydeau's success is as much visual as anything else. (Of course he hasn't one fraction of Miss Brophy's other talents.)

I do wish I had seen this play. It should have been delectably played and directed – it needed a very great deal of charm in the players, and this might have compensated for the relatively uninteresting visual aspect.

I remember some pretty tough notices, but I didn't read them in detail at the time (I think I was in Boston during the week it opened). In addition, no one in their senses would present this play at the Vaudeville. It needed a theatre like the Criterion, I imagine.

So, I will read the new play. I have the feeling that Miss Brophy is far too intelligent to write another play in a quasi-naturalistic style, but I only hope she hasn't gone too far in the other direction (this is what usually happens)!

But whatever her new play may be like (and I shall read it tonight) she must be cherished by somebody, because she could become a formidable playwright. Prejudice against anyone (and she seems to have collected some) is very easily swept aside. This is part of an agent's job, when selling a play, as you know.

Best regards,

yours,

18 September 1968

Dear Brigid,

I hope you don't think I am being slack. Frank Dunlop opens his play tomorrow, and I want specially to talk to him personally about your play [Love Now, Die Later], because if we want the National Theatre it has to go to Tynan unless we can somehow fix it with Frank. I remember you said that you and Tynan were not lovers at Oxford.

I am still becoming an expert on Brophy and hope to emerge unscathed.

Ever yours,

CARYL CHURCHILL

*

John McGrath, a Ramsay client for a couple of years, saw a student production of a play by Churchill (1938–), another Oxford undergraduate, and put her in touch with Ramsay. Churchill sent her a stage play and a television play, which she had also sent to another agent.

7 December 1961

Dear Caryl,

I think you are very difficult to sell, because your writing is in some respects very slight and poetic (this isn't meant disparagingly in the least). I am sure this wouldn't be a handicap on radio, but it's a real one on television. In an odd kind of way you are getting more fey and more esoteric, instead of blunter and sturdier, which is not what I expected1 Have you thought of writing a novel, or a children's book? I have the feeling that you would find it easier,

Best regards,

15 March 1962

Dear Caryl,

I do hope some other agents turned up [*to the Experimental Theatre Club performances of Churchill's* Easy Death, *Oxford Playhouse*] and that they are really keen to try and help you. I think you need very sympathetic and careful representing, and in some ways it might be better for you to have a male agent, since women tend to find their own weaknesses in their own sex. For instance, I found the production at Oxford too tenuous and over-lyrical, whereas you need strong, anti-feminine interpretation.

Warm regards, yours,

Ramsay sold a radio play to the BBC, which broadcast it in November 1962. Churchill had married and was a mother and was not able to focus full-time on her writing, in which she was experimenting with time, masks and puppets, often to Ramsay's bewilderment. After selling more radio plays to the BBC in the late 1960s, Ramsay managed to interest Michael Codron in Churchill's work and his commission, Owners, *was produced at the Royal Court's Theatre Upstairs in 1972. It was her first professional stage work. Churchill became Resident Dramatist at the Court in the mid-1970s and had her earliest major plays produced there. She stayed with Ramsay until Ramsay's death.*

25 March 1963

Dear Caryl,

I think one can – almost – write a play in a trance – provided one has the rarest and most extraordinary genius. For the rest, I'm sure that playwriting – unlike Zen – must have a deep inner meaning, if it hasn't a clear surface one.

Ever yours,

25 January 1983

Dear Caryl,

As I warned you, any Play that is shown to Max [*Stafford-Clark, Royal Court Artistic Director*] is in a trap. This is a pity, because one ought to explore the possibility of the Royal Court and Max, but one shouldn't be like a fly in a trap just by sending a Play or talking about a Play. If only he would allow an Author to give a Play freely, and not make it a kind of blackmail! Due to this, Bond will never ever ever again give any Play to the Royal Court while Max is at that theatre, which I think is very sad, as the Court is an ideal stage for Bond's plays, rather than some place like the Cottesloe – but the National doesn't exercise the kind of power over a Play which Max personally exercises.

This letter is not an attack on Max, who really needs a psychiatrist to eliminate this flaw.

Yours,

RICHARD COTTRELL

*

Cottrell (1936–) wrote Deutsches Haus, *one of the student plays John Barton presented, and which Ramsay saw, at Cambridge in 1959. She agreed to represent him, and the play with its undergraduate cast came to the Arts Theatre, London. Cottrell continued to write and adapt but little to Ramsay's satisfaction, and from the mid-1960s he concentrated on directing.*

14 December 1966

Dear Richard,

A ROOM WITH A VIEW

I have trotted through what you are pleased to call a "working draft script". I thought you had begun this task months ago, but if you are only at the draft stage, is it worth it? Why not write a play and be done with it?

The text is full of super things, but your first few pages make my spirits plummet visual-wise! What on earth are you going to unveil to us as the curtain rises? A stage cluttered with nooks – a bit of the Sistine Chapel (small backcloth), another area with a man sitting reading a paper, then a dining room with several obligatory small tables, then the drawing room. Does this mean a stage chopped up into horrible little areas, with actors huddling into them as the scenes change?

Yes, it's a "draft", but do, clever and talented little boy that you are, realise that NO adaptation should take more than, say, two months of your time to complete. It's a matter of intelligence, mechanics and professionalism. If it's taking you months, and you end up with a working draft script you should begin to question whether you are really apt as an adaptor. Balzac could have written La Comédie Humaine in that time.

Are you a <u>real adaptor</u>, or do you just want to be?????

I am harsh because you have so much talent and sensibility and intelligence, and I don't find that working draft script solves what must be a difficult but superhumanly difficult task.

Fondly,

DAVID CREGAN

Cregan (1931–2015) joined Ramsay in the mid-1960s when a member of the Royal Court's Writers' Group, which included other Ramsay clients Edward Bond and Ann Jellicoe.

9 December 1969

Dear David,

You're never going to be successful while you continue to hate people who are successful and passionately desire success yourself.

The curious thing is that one gets practically everything when one has ceased to want it. This isn't a trick, it is merely that when one wants something very badly, one doesn't set out to get it very well.

Love as ever,

9 December 1971

Dear David,

A really good play ought to seem enormously simple and one should say to oneself, why has no-one ever written this before?

Much love,

Dear Cregan,

I find the whole discussion of success sordid, ugly and fruitless. Perhaps in my snobbish way I think it's something which "they" talk about, and it's not something that people who create even consider. Success, such as it is, is gained by not trying to get it. It turns out to be a killer because it disturbs and destroys peoples' lives, and eats away into their working time. You're a success one season, and twenty other people are a success the next. It has had a disastrous effect on people like Osborne and Wesker and hundreds of others. Please don't raise this subject again, David, for your sake, not mine.

Much love,

JONATHAN GEMS

*

Gems (1952–) was one of a younger generation of playwrights to join Ramsay in the late 1970s when she felt it increasingly difficult to keep in touch with developments in the theatre. She was still thrilled to welcome new talent, but the turnover in clients was becoming higher than before. Gems stayed from 1977 until 1982.

6 October 1982

My dear Johnny,

I am really tired of authors passing the buck about it being everyone else's fault they didn't totally succeed, because they have a considerable amount of talent themselves. Talent isn't enough; <u>work and self-criticism</u> is essential.

Yours,

PETER GILL

*

Gill (1939–) joined Ramsay in 1969, the year he directed his own plays Over Gardens Out *and* The Sleepers' Den *at the Royal Court Theatre Upstairs. He was then known for his productions of D. H. Lawrence's plays before his reputation as a playwright came to match that of his directing.*

5 November 1973

My dear Peter,

Just to wish you great good fortune with THE MERRY-GO-ROUND. Do you think D.H. Lawrence dropped in and saw CHARLEY'S AUNT when he was half way through this play, because his ending is exactly the same?!

With love and luck,

CHRISTOPHER HAMPTON

*

While an undergraduate at Oxford University, Hampton (1946–) had his play When Did You Last See My Mother? *staged at the Oxford Playhouse, and the administrator there suggested he approach Ramsay. He stayed with Ramsay until her death.*

Dear Christopher Hampton,

<u>WHEN DID YOU LAST SEE MY MOTHER?</u>

Yes, I found your play very interesting, and Liz [*Sweeting, Oxford Playhouse administrator*] has written to me today to say that she will allow me to show it to Michael Codron.

Of course the length of this play isn't a length possible in the ordinary way in the professional theatre, but I would like Michael to see it, because he is just taking over a long lease hold on the Fortune Theatre (the theatre where BEYOND THE FRINGE ran for so long). This is a theatre which could do things somewhat off beat. In addition, Bill Gaskill of the Royal Court has asked me to have a long talk with Michael Codron so that they might do something together. The Royal Court is going through a desperately hard time with no money and a rather bad choice of plays. A copy of your play would simply moulder at the Court during the next few weeks, but the Court would be a very good place for your kind of play.

The other person likely to be interested in your play is Michael White who is, at the moment, in management with Oscar Lewenstein. White's problem is that though he has superb taste, he hates parting with money, and it's almost impossible to get an Option out of him.

The third possibility for this play is to show it to Jim Haynes of the Traverse Theatre Edinburgh. The Traverse are just about to take a small theatre in London called the Jeanetta Cochrane Theatre, which they will rename. There isn't really any other outlet for small plays of this sort at the moment. The Arts Theatre is simply an empty shell hired for money, and no discerning Manager hires the Arts anymore, because the public have ceased to go to the theatre due to mismanagement.

When you next come to London, do come in and see me. The last Oxford author we took on while he was still a student was David Rudkin, who sent me several plays while he was still a student, and who wrote AFORE NIGHT COME just before he came down. David has had a curiously interesting career in London. After AFORE NIGHT COME at the Arts and Aldwych, Peter Hall commissioned him to do the text of the Schoenberg libretto for Covent Garden. He has written two outstanding television plays (one is still to be televised), and Peter Brook is hoping that David will write a film for him. Meanwhile, David has just been working on the Truffaut text for his new film being shot in London at the moment.

Very much depends on how long you are staying at Oxford, what you wish to do afterwards, and how you are "financially placed", as they say. You will find the work you write at Oxford is unlikely to be the best work you will write, and if you can manage to work slowly and steadily developing all the time you will go much further than if you try to run too fast and get labelled as a scrappy immature author by the London critics. The criticisms they hand out at Oxford are always warm and more kindly than they give to a play in a professional theatre. Sometimes they do harm to authors by over-praising them too early, and three or four authors who made their debut at Cambridge a few years ago with very promising plays have now sunk like stones. It is really not just a matter of talent – it is a matter of character as well.

Looking forward to meeting you.

Sincerely yours,

30 June 1966

Dear Helen [*Montagu, Royal Court general manager*],

Christopher can't take on any commissioning, but he would love to write you a play when he can. The point is that he is going to try and get a First Degree in Modern Languages. His tutor says there is a faint chance if he works awfully hard, and he is determined to try. I very much like this side of Christopher – of course he would like to be commissioned, and of course he would like to have £100, but I think this desire to do something tremendously well is going to give us great pleasure when he concentrates entirely on playwriting when he leaves Oxford. He is hoping to live in Germany next year and his tutor knows some theatre, I think it is in Hamburg. This would be marvellous for him because he could be in a town working on his German and also seeing a great deal of theatre. If the Court has any links to Germany, perhaps you might care to talk to Christopher about this?

Each time I meet him I am more impressed by him. I like his disinterest in success and his interest in work. It will be awfully nice if the play runs for more than three weeks, or even if it were to be very successful for three weeks. I have told him that failure is just as interesting an experience as success, so he is prepared for anything.

Warm regards,

ever yours,

DAVID HARE

*

When Hare (1947–) joined Ramsay in 1973, he was Resident Dramatist at the Nottingham Playhouse, where Brassneck, *co-authored with Howard Brenton, would open that September. Hare was known as founder of, and writer for, the alternative Portable Theatre and for his association with the Royal Court, which had staged* Slag *in 1970. On reading Hare's new play* Knuckle, *his agent Clive Goodwin thought it a wrong turn. Taking Christopher Hampton's advice, Hare sent the play to Ramsay, who read it overnight and adored it. With Ramsay's support, Michael Codron, who had commissioned the play, planned to bring it into the West End, a first foray for Hare and the start of his close relationship with Ramsay that lasted until her death.*

[undated, late 1973; handwritten]

Dear David,

'Success' and 'failure' mean <u>nothing</u>. What matters is true talent, and the exercise of the talent.

I've not learned much about life but I have learned that if one allows fear to stop one doing anything, then one must throw in the sponge.

Yours,

113

Rehearsals of Knuckle *were scheduled to begin at the end of December*
1973.

13 November 1973

Dear Hare,

I've just talked to Richard Eyre [*Artistic Director, Nottingham Playhouse*],
who phoned me. He says he thinks you're awfully scared about KNUCKLE
and a possible flop. Of course you probably are, but one CANNOT run
away from these things. If you want to be completely at ease, you must write
the William Douglas-Home style of play – well made shit.

Yes, failure is POSSIBLE – so what? J Joyce failed, Beckett starved,
CARMEN flopped (too avant-garde), Proust was turned down by Gide
and his group. Dostoyevsky starved; all the early Chekhovs and Ibsens failed
ignominiously. But they didn't withdraw their plays, they got performed and
ended up immortal. Just pin your ears back and let Michael Cod operate.
If they don't follow it, if it doesn't make its money back at the box office, it
cannot possibly do you or your career any harm. Richard spoke about his
desperate failure in the W.E. and his anguish. But the Ann Jellicoe play [The
Giveaway] was a piece of rubbish which turned out not be to be funny on
the night. The failure was chiefly due to the fact that people (critics) believed
Ann to be an intellectual, whereas she's just a girl with a fringe. You must
OPERATE as a writer, neither success nor failure of this play will harm you.
I will be the one to have Clive [*Goodwin*] crowing – think of poor little me.
Whereas I say fuck Clive and his policy of no-risks. ONLY risks will drive
you forward. If they aren't risks, they aren't any good.

I'm glad you're off out of London for December. The theatre is a terrible
bore as a diet. It can only be taken in short concentrated doses – you've had
FAR too much. I hardly ever think about the theatre. If I wasn't "in" it, I'd
go about four times a year (if that). People who go every night are punch
drunk with its mediocrity.

Everyone who is connected with the play LOVES it. So – let's enjoy it
all. You are creating some kind of non-existent shadowy bogey, and it will
deplete you unless you conquer this.

114

I don't have any particular judgment about things, but I have a kind of intuition and we have had an enormous proportion of successes with the plays we've represented. Just luck, but in fact it's because we on the whole only represent plays by <u>really talented people</u>, and there's a kind of rough justice, from the press.

Following a two-week run in Oxford, the London opening was unexpectedly delayed and Hare became increasingly anxious.

15 February 1974

Dear Hare,

Yes, it <u>is true</u> that KNUCKLE is complex – <u>"Curly"</u> is complex – nobody else. How much is bravado? Like you, he's a fierce puritan, but probably too young to know what he's doing <u>logically</u>, though we know what he sets out to do. But he remains something of a puzzle, and somehow doesn't <u>want</u> us to intrude. There's quite a bit of you in Curly and I bet you puzzle people too (the way Chris [*Hampton*] doesn't puzzle them!) and you want it that way, partly because you can't bear intrusion (quite right), and partly because you don't <u>know</u> yourself (who does?) and because you are, perhaps, piling all sorts of handicaps on yourself, like a racehorse.

It doesn't matter about <u>your</u> enigma, because we aren't being ASKED to understand. But a character in a play must, I suppose, be understood, or be clearly shown to be someone trying to obstruct being known. But I don't mind not quite understanding all of "Curly". I spent some years (or was it weeks?) married to a psychiatrist and oh the <u>boredom</u> of knowing everything. I now make no effort to analyse anymore, and just live by a vague, sawney intuition.

All I must recommend to you, without intrusion, is the Alexander Principle – first read my book. Second, if you believe it can cure your asthma (which it certainly can), you need to find a practitioner and have a course. It seems to me a complex course, but even taking the advice on posture and relaxation has given me endless extra energy and freedom from even a backache.

Knuckle *opened in London at the Comedy Theatre on 4 March 1974.*

5 March 1974

Dear David,

I've had to turn to the typewriter because the letter I've written has such a neurotic handwriting that I can't even read it.

It's no good Max [*Stafford-*]Clark talking about "uncommercial" plays only going on at a subsidized theatre!! You were offered two weeks in a crummy season at the Court – would that have been better? Or did you want to do a return trip to Hampstead [*which had staged Hare's* The Great Exhibition] and stay there for the rest of your career?

As long as you can get a Management to spend £30,000 on one of your plays, you can bet you are one of the peak writers and one of the lucky ones. The Court trundle on play after play, usually ignoring the really talented ones. Most of the Court would give their eye-teeth to have a Manager like Codron proud and happy to do a play of theirs.

FUCK the critics. They've all compromised or sold out. They are failures. And along comes a shining child of 26 and tells them what's wrong with them. They aren't big enough to take the blows. Are you really going to allow these grey shabby lot break your spirit and your confidence? EVERYONE has knocks. Ibsen was a disaster for years. So was Chekhov. But more and more people began understanding their work and demanding them. Have you read Ibsen's Life? You'd better do so because you can see that fame of his sort required years of accepted suffering.

All that matters is your work. No, not absolutely all. Because you mustn't treat yourself as a person so harshly. It's all inverted conceit, in an odd sort of way. Look OUTWARD, my dear child. Don't muck about picking at your entrails, and shitting on yourself. Your work is more important than you are because it's what everybody can actually hear and see. You have great talent and are mucking about by trying to destroy your nerve. The only way you will get failure is to deliberately bring it on yourself.

As for the play at the Comedy: you happen to have [*Edward*] Fox, not Scofield. Your notices are far better than SAVAGES…it's just to get the people IN. Even after excellent notices for Ayckbourn [Absurd Person Singular] at the Cri[*terion*], nobody came for around ten days. Michael [Codron] was frantic and kept saying he didn't understand why wonderful notices didn't bring in the public. We shall see what happens. I just don't know. But I am one of a great number of people, increasing all the time, who believe in your quite outstanding talent. Both you and Margaret [*Matheson, then his wife*] have a group of people who would do anything to help you and encourage you both – if you stay together, or if you decide to stay apart. We liked it when you were together, but that's up to you both.

What those grey old failures hated was your passion and your youth, which shine out of that bloody super romantic confection which is just about to give its next performance to the public, hundreds of whom will love it. I wish you'd have heard the hush with which the first night audience listened to your play. I was swept overboard by it, and am sorry you missed it. I shall go and see it continuously. As I said on the phone, nobody of the critics mentioned that the characters were 'off stage', nobody mentioned the way you conveyed the intricacies of the plot SO well. The whole play held. But they couldn't take some of the contents. Eddie's speech in a paper-bag, for instance. It was too close, at the present time, since all of us are responsible for the way the country has gone to hell. Greedy and vengeful people everywhere. Of course they prefer some old fashioned bromide. But we HAVE to try and break through and not run away to the subsidized theatres. It will be easier next for you and for others.

But try and get it into your head that there are truly concerned and friendly people who care a lot about you, and about Margaret, and don't care to see both of you suffering during this crisis. We know we can't help, but we are THERE.

So that's all for tonight, Life's Delicate Child (as Thomas Mann called your like).

Dear David,

This is written from home at 6 am on Wednesday the 6th – a time of day when truth stares one in the face. <u>So</u> badly written it had to be copied and doesn't seem much of a letter, in type; what a dawn aberration.

Now, you either believe that the theatre is important, or you don't. If you do, then you tell the truth on the stage and expect <u>to be listened to</u>. Your play attacks capitalism, and says that the City is corrupt. You say that England is now a place of dishonour. You say this in the heart of the West End, to people who have all had to compromise or sell-out in order to get where they are – the rich first-nighters and the British <u>press</u>.

When you find that these people <u>don't</u> want to let other people hear what you are saying, you – and the rest of us – say it's because the play isn't 'commercial' and should have been tucked away in a small out-of-the-way hall. Hampstead, R. Court. It's like a revolutionary who has the opportunity of blowing up Parliament saying <u>if only</u> he'd blown up Dewsbury Town Hall he'd have got away with it.

YOU ARE RESPONSIBLE for what you write and you must take the consequences. You have said things in the West End which have never been said before, and you expect to have the notices which greet a well-made play with French windows. Of course the men who are hired by our National Press are going to consider their own jobs. They are hired helps of perhaps the most disgusting Press we have ever had.

You are writing a play attacking what that audience and that Press <u>live by</u>. They do their best to get the play removed by typical means – they ignore the message and savage the package.

You can't be a simple West End success <u>and</u> launch an attack of this sort. You don't have to be a Tory to repudiate it. The attack you make <u>is total</u>. You say these things and then <u>don't want them heard</u>. Then you disappear to Nottingham having refused to sit through the first night. David, you have to face the firing squad if you want to change the world.

Those Arab and Israeli revolutionaries – and the Irish ones – stand up and say "We did this because we want to change the world". There are a number of people dead and a number of people in jail for doing something and standing firm. The <u>word</u> is as powerful as a bomb, but we choose not to allow ourselves to believe it.

Max Clark is, of course, right when he says "Why didn't you attack in Dewsbury? or in the <u>permitted</u> area of Hyde Park where orators are allowed to speak revolution." The capitalist system of the theatre paid for your attack. The only person who is running away <u>is the author</u>. But you can't run away, because you have <u>written the words</u> which can be heard <u>8 times a week</u>.

Let's all be calm and try and keep the play going. You have to live <u>through</u> the pain, David, and you'll come out on the other side, so Gide tells one!

6 March 1974

Dear Mr [*Edward*] Fox,

I hope you don't mind an agent unknown to you (David's) writing this letter.

Don't let the Critics triumph by letting what they say destroy the playing of it.

In the heart of Capitalist London, a tiny group (paid for by Capitalist backing) are denouncing it and telling everyone that our nation is in decay, leading a life of dishonour. Some of the people who love the play have said we should have sought the sanctuary of a subsidised theatre (the Court or Hampstead) but even Guy Fawkes wouldn't still be celebrated if he had chosen to blow up Surbiton Cricket Club instead of Parliament; nor would he have died for it.

Every night, you and your cast stand up and say what we all believe should be said. Don't allow these petty and venal men to spoil or disturb your beautifully relaxed, breath-taking performance, or those of your superb cast.

Every night during the run some hundreds of people will come, and even if they are quiet (and I myself am an entirely silent audience), you must tell them the secret about life which is implicit in this play; that we are all alone, but all together, and we must stand firm and not sell out, and we must be brave.

All good wishes,

Dear Irving [*Wardle*, Times *critic*],

What's wrong with an author who translates British life into fairyland?

I don't remember your complaining about Orton – he was apparently permitted. And poor old Barrie wouldn't have been able to afford his Whitehall Court residence if you'd been around (and I don't mean PETER PAN). And what about literature? Firbank would be "out". For art – goodbye Edward Lear. All these people saw people through their own eyes and wrote or drew them seriously. Hare's "Curly" is a perfectly serious drawing of a YOUNG man. Marked by "literature" (which includes [*Ross*] Macdonald and [*Mickey*] Spillane), very idealistic and romantic and savage, because he is a puritan.

I fear the critics are neither young, nor puritans, so it is difficult for them. (I hear Harold [*Hobson*] had his entire collection of pornography stolen from his flat – Orton's diary just escaped.)

Well, it will soon be an all-revival West End, and the critics will be re-assessing the judgements of Hazlitt and Agate. With a bit of luck, those of us who actually wish to find, develop and nurture outstanding new writers will have long turned to a more life-enhancing occupation.

Love,

PS: What about Stoppard and Barnes?

JOHN HOLMSTROM
(A.K.A. ROGER GELLERT)

*

In her first year as an agent, Ramsay represented five plays that were broadcast on radio, including two translations by Holmstrom (1927–2013), with whom she became close friends. He was working as a radio announcer when he met Ramsay and in the 1960s he briefly joined her as a script reader. Using the name Roger Gellert, he wrote one play, Quaint Honour, *in which a public school prefect seduces a junior boy, a scandalous subject for the time. She secured a production in 1958 at the Arts Theatre, London under club conditions.*

Monday *[undated, 1953]*

Dear John,

I was glad to hear that you liked The Deep Blue Sea, as it is really in that <u>direction</u> that authors should write for the stage. By that, I mean the reality behind the façade. Where Rattigan was so wise was to take an ordinary woman – and an Englishwoman at that – and show her clearly under the strain of an obsession. And this kind of obsession is far more potent and dangerous than mere drug taking or other vices.

Yesterday, in a bus, I saw a man with a very pretty and <u>very</u> ordinary young woman. And near them I saw a young girl, very plain, looking at them, the kind of young girl this man would never look at twice. But how extraordinarily foolish of these men to be taken in by these pretty good-time girls, when there are these quiet, plain girls full of extraordinary possibilities of feeling, due to their secret dreams and imaginings. I think someone should write a play on a plain young woman, who fulfils herself through dreams. And the astonishment of the young man if he were to allow himself to become entangled with such a nature.

Your agent,

PS. Rattigan always loves "inferior" boys and I'm sure this makes him behave very badly (self-disgust etc.) – this is why he was able to show that woman [*Hester in* The Deep Blue Sea] as <u>unlike herself as it was possible to be</u>. This brings the recognition-amazement I think is so essential to playwriting.

Wednesday *[undated, 1953]*

Dear John,

How neatly you type! The trouble about your fragment of truth is that I can't ever grasp a <u>condition</u>. This is what makes me good with plays, because in a play a <u>general condition</u> means exactly bugger nothing! It's not in the least important that you should be so far denied the "usual" experiences – they bring nothing with them. It is only what <u>you bring</u> which makes them important at all. One simply creates a person and then lavishes one's feelings upon them, or lashes oneself into misery, because that is what is required by one's innermost being.

Gide is really the man for you – he says that everything comes with its own need. And I couldn't agree more. But one must be "available" for life. (Gide himself wasn't available until well after 30.)

Rattigan has skill and sensibility, but he's really awfully "ordinary". Whiting is far more interesting, but he seems to write in a kind of dream and never breaks through the curtain sharply enough for us. I've read Marching Song and like it, but it <u>isn't enough</u> – I mean the whole thing is too "watered", as it were. And therefore it partially fails. But his Saint's Day was very revealing in its imagery.

Your school play [Quaint Honour] will be most interesting, I feel. And there's nothing to worry about when it comes to limited "experience". There are millions of people going through the full cycle of life up to the hilt, but who could not give us one single piece of information which might give us a better understanding of what it's all about.

Have you read "Death in Venice"? – that really wonderful story of Mann's about his obsession for a beautiful young boy in Venice? If not, I have a copy.

Your Agent,

DONALD HOWARTH

*

Howarth (1931–) joined Ramsay in 1959, the year his play Lady on the Barometer, *which had been seen as a Sunday night production without décor at the Royal Court the year before, was revived as a main Court production, renamed* Sugar in the Morning.

Dear Donald,

I feel awfully worried about your future, and what you are going to do to earn a decent living. The trouble is that you are writing so sporadically, and at the moment there is only one play [All Good Children] of yours to sell, which you wrote ages and ages ago, and have been many many months in re-writing.

It seems to me that you are wanting to combine acting, Directing, and writing all together, and if this is the case, I really urge you to put your eggs in one basket, and get an agent who deals <u>with them all.</u>

As you know, I don't look after actors or Directors and <u>I don't want to.</u>

You know we shall always be friends, and I shall always be more than pleased to read and criticise your plays and give you any help possible.

Love,

Howarth stayed with Ramsay and continued to direct as well as write.

3 March 1967

Dear Donald,

To say that a text can't be judged from a text makes nonsense of my job. A play agent's job is to judge a text, but the judgement isn't based on rules – it is based on emotion, intuition and faith. It isn't like the photograph of a painting or the score of a symphony – to read a script is to imagine what could be.

Love,

3 February 1969

Dear Donald,

I've read THE APPOINTMENT [*which became* Three Months Gone], which I certainly prefer to the last two you wrote, although I'm not <u>bowled over</u> by it.

I'm wondering really whether this removal of the censor [*in 1968*] is going to yield better plays. You're certainly able to tell more of the truth, yet in a way, the discipline of censorship made you write LILY [A Lily in Little India], which is, on the whole, a better play than this one, in which you have indulged yourself a bit more. It's enabled you to be more <u>labyrinthine</u>, but I'm not quite <u>sure</u> if this is an advantage.

Anyway, this shows signs of <u>hard work</u>, which appeals to me.

I read a lot of plays during the weekend, so I'll try and take this away and read it again, and maybe I'll find more virtues in it than I seem to have found so far!!!!

You must laugh when you get a letter from me, because I never seem to have been known to praise, have I? The poor authors I represent certainly go through the hoop!

Love as ever,

9 December 1969

Dear Donald,

I hope you are not still churning over in your mind this business of the Court's responsibility towards playwrights. On the whole the Court do more for playwrights than any other theatre. When I said that authors could work in other media like TV, radio, poetry and fiction I was trying to say I didn't think authors could be treated in any way differently from actors. Actors too have to earn their living apart from the stage because it seems as if the public don't support the theatre sufficiently to keep all the actors and playwrights alive. I think some of this is the fault of everyone in the theatre who isn't sufficiently enthusiastic. If we become apathetic, the public is going to be apathetic.

Love,

Ramsay's father came from a Jewish family but converted to Christianity in South Africa when Ramsay was a child. Many of her clients supported the cultural boycott, though a few, while opposed to apartheid, wanted to make a difference by having their work performed, preferably to non-segregated audiences (a condition impossible to guarantee).

Dear Donald,

I can't write to you while you are in that country [*South Africa*], living with people who permit such terrible things to happen while they bask in luxury, which they hug to themselves, denying freedom of any sort to so many thousands, whose only fault is a mere difference in the pigmentation of their skin.

I note that you think your friends depriving these selfish and vulgar self-appointed "elite" of their plays is "negative", uncreative and odious – like apartheid.

I read last week about the police holding a man by his feet from a high building in Johannesburg and just dropping him – rather creative, really, isn't it?

Love,

2 November 1971

Dear Donald,

I wrote you a pretty unhelpful letter yesterday, but I find the S.A. regime so dreadful that I find it almost impossible to be calm.

In your long letter you sneered at all the good authors who tried to express their distaste by saying they did not wish their plays to be done in a country which supports the present regime. Their selfless sacrifice (because every author longs to communicate, it is why he [*sic*] is an author), has done a very great deal in criticising that country and the country has become deeply concerned about the ban. It is only by changing the conscience of the people (and in the case of S.A. challenging their superiority and importance) that one can influence them to throw out a government which makes them a disgusting spectacle in the eyes of concerned people in the rest of the world.

When I was in Africa, their hatred and contempt was turned on the Jews – not the rich successful ones who changed their names and pretended they weren't Jewish, but the ordinary innocent Jew. I attended a school where nobody in any class was prepared to talk to a Jew – "yids", they were called, because they were "irreverent". Now the yids have become successful, so they are okay. Gandhi was persecuted early in his career in Durban because he was an Indian – different, humble, poor. This is what started him on is selfless career.

I expect the people of the country are not much worse than we are – the anti-black movement here is appalling. BUT AT LEAST THE GOVERNMENT – THE ELECTED GOVERNMENT (Labour, Tory and Liberal) are all declared enemies of discrimination, and punishment is built in our laws if we practice discrimination. In South Africa, the opposite prevails – one is punished if one is liberal and concerned. One of the great men of Africa, Mandela, is in gaol.

I do not think you and Arnold [*Wesker*] are right, but I am quite sure that you are not doing this for your own ends. It is certainly being used as approval of S.A.

Jennie [*Wright*] in this office, who typed yesterday's letter, pointed out that our government's behaviour in Ireland is based on unequal principles and we should do something about this. I quite agree.

Love,

ANN JELLICOE

*

Jellicoe (1927–2017) first met Ramsay in the mid-1950s when she wanted to present Büchner's Danton's Death *at the Cockpit Theatre, London, which she had founded. Ramsay fought hard for her to use a translation by one of her clients. When a little later Jellicoe wrote her first full-length play,* The Sport of My Mad Mother, *and needed an agent, she thought Ramsay might fight for her work just as vigorously. They had a stormy relationship.*

Dear Ann,

I am enchanted by the remark that you feel uneasy without my familiar weaknesses! I must tell you that I am always drawn to people by their weaknesses and their faults because of course, I recognise anybody's weaknesses and faults as my own. But then surely we are all everything, and it is all a matter of degree and balance – one must just try to slightly balance towards strength rather than weaknesses – but it is almost impossible not to make a mistake occasionally.

What a splendid idea to have the audience drinking wine and perhaps nibbling something. When I was tiny, on Saturday mornings we used to play hookey from school and go to the town's cinema-cafe where one could watch a film and have a snack at the same time. I have always longed for this in both the cinema and the theatre. [*Royal Court Theatre*] Upstairs is just perfect for such an occasion.

Love,

THOMAS KILROY

*

Ramsay agreed to represent Kilroy (1934–) in 1967 when he sent her his first play, The O'Neill. *He stayed until her death. In 1968, with a new play,* The Death and Resurrection of Mr Roche, *being produced in Dublin, he asked her to suggest a New York agent and, among others, she mentioned Lucy Kroll.*

3 December 1968

Dear Tom,

I shall try and phone you tonight, but meanwhile I feel I must write and say a few things.

First, an author <u>employs</u> an agent, and instructs an agent what he wants: an agent doesn't own a play, and shouldn't be allowed to behave as if she or he does.

When Michael [*Codron*] phoned me to say that he would dearly love to present ROCHE in London, I told him that when Miss Kroll appeared in Dublin, you had handed the play over to her, and she had deliberately avoided getting in touch with me, as she wanted the whole thing for herself. You in your turn agreed, because you thought she had more to offer, and you were afraid that if you had stood by me you might have lost something by it. She flew to Dublin because of a notice by a British critic in a New York Paper, and being a ruthless and ambitious agent, she now wants to manipulate your talent and insist that you will sell it to the highest bidder – as if the theatre were a cattle market, and if money now was the only thing that mattered. This is the way to destroy an author's future and an author's reputation.

No single really good author I know would put the money offered him <u>before</u> the artistic necessities, since money uneerily [*unerringly?*] follows artistic achievement.

I don't care a damn if I represent your play or not. If Michael does it I will be happy to offer him backing for it to go on. If you need money now, I shall be happy to lend you, say, £500 without strings. But if all you want is to be treated like some kind of commodity sold on the market for the highest price, there's no more to be said.

Michael has been instrumental in launching dozens of careers, and dozens of authors and stars owe their careers to him (Pinter, for instance, to name one of a dozen famous authors). The boy who wrote [There's] A GIRL IN MY SOUP has made so much money that he has to live in exile in Italy to keep a proportion of it. His success – so quick and so sudden, with all that rush of money, will undoubtedly destroy his career as a playwright for some years. He hasn't written anything worth doing since.

To write well and live in honour and self-respect: not to sell out, or betray – this isn't difficult if you allow yourself to think about what you need from life and what you owe to those close to you.

Best regards,

Dear Tom,

When an author has his lawyer it always takes twice or even three times as long, because the lawyers are lawyers first and knowledgeable about the theatre a <u>very long way behind</u>.

Dear Tom,

Michael, in spite of being small, frail and quiet, has great tenacity, but does need warm and concerned handling by us all. I don't find this difficult, as he never annoys me, is always available, works very hard, and most important of all, has really good taste allied to genuine modesty. He hasn't changed in the least from when I first met him at the beginning of his career. Mark you, this metier is so hard and so hurtful from time to time, that people who survive in it do so by a kind of stoical endurance, and if possible, the retention of some kind of inner life. There is not much happiness from the career itself, except hard work, which is a good disciplinary hair-shirt for us all!

Theatres are all doing very badly at the moment – and everyone seems very down and distracted. It's a temporary malaise, like the flu (only worse) since you can't escape to bed. Tonight I'm going to a ridiculous first night of FUNNY GIRL, Streisand is coming over, and the Producer, Ray Stark, has engineered a Royal Opening – I can't tell you the horror of this kind of thing. Everyone in full evening dress, standing like dummies worshipping Royalty, if you please. This is followed by a gala dinner at Claridges, which I'm going to duck. This film will be a big success, of course.

Best,

Dear Tom,

THE DEATH AND RESURRECTION OF MR ROCHE

Of course, I wanted you to read Peter Hall's remarks, but please don't for one moment imagine that he has some special gift or authority for judging plays. He has, in his time, fallen very flat on his face from various plays which he has chosen.

The really interesting thing about the history of any play, is the astonishing remarks and rejections which it receives before it goes on. The only plays which get unanimous praise and which get on with the greatest ease, are those that sink like stones. Any good original talent, should have something slightly daunting about it, even ugly, certainly not acceptable to everybody, or it wouldn't be new.

The Peter Barnes play [The Ruling Class] suffers from being transferred from the provinces. Nobody does any work to make it better. A provincial play looks wonderful in the home town, and curiously provincial in London, unless it is re-thought.

The Orton play at Brighton [What the Butler Saw] seems to be getting worse rather than better, but as there was a crisis about it, I think the Managers do know that the actors must be allowed to relax and bloom and make the play an entertainment.

We had a play opening in New York last night, and we haven't heard anything about how it's going. It's still at the preview stage, so I suppose nobody knows until the critics tell them!

Best regards,

STEPHEN LOWE

*

Lowe (1947–) was starting out as a writer and working with Alan Ayckbourn in Scarborough when he approached Ramsay in September 1976; he left Ramsay six years later.

28 October 1976

Dear Stephen,

I don't see why the [*Royal Court*] Theatre Upstairs is aiming too high. I know it has about 150 steps, but that's the only consideration of height.

Best wishes,

FRANK MARCUS

*

Marcus (1926–96) was introduced to Ramsay by a mutual friend in the early 1960s and stayed with the agency until her death.

21 November 1966

Dear Michael [*Codron*],

I can't think of a tattier way of selling [The Killing of] SISTER GEORGE than to sell it to Bette Davis. I think she is an old-fashioned, out-of-date actress who does old-fashioned ghastly films. I know Frank wants to write his own Screenplay, but I only wish that he would allow someone else to do it, and tell the relationship between SISTER GEORGE and CHILDIE before the film starts. I think we could have a quite extraordinary success if we were to tell the first meeting of SISTER GEORGE and CHILDIE, and how she managed to get rid of Childie's young man, and the play is only the last twenty minutes of the film.

Love,

JOHN McGRATH

*

McGrath (1935–02) came to Ramsay in 1958 while studying at Oxford University. He left her and returned again in 1965 and then stayed with her until her death.

19 November 1965

Dear John,

EVENTS WHILE GUARDING THE BOFORS GUN

I shall have to steal myself to read any play with a background of war. For about twenty years I was in love with everything to do with war, and as is the way with love, it doesn't last! I am now dreadfully weary of all war backgrounds, but I will try and take this in my stride when I am reading your play.

Love,

16 May 1966

Dear John,

Sam S.[*Spiegel*] has great charm, but be careful, he is a real corruptor in the most diabolical way. He is the nearest thing to Mephistopheles I have ever met.

Much love,

16 October 1968

Dear John,

I have been sent all sorts of cuttings from New York about [*Herbert*] Marcuse, which seem to have got mislaid before I've even had a chance to read them. When I was in New York in February, I scoured the bookshops to get Marcuse books; consequently everybody I met in New York sends me cuttings of Marcuse as if he's my fiancé or something. I hope I find the cuttings because they might be of interest to you.

EROS AND CIVILISATION I found splendid, but the last book he wrote, which has been published in England in hardback, I found almost unreadable.

The name Langston Hughes rings no bells. I take it that I am the only person capable of reading who has not heard of Langston Hughes? You had better tell me who he is so that I may be suitably ashamed for not knowing.

Love,

DAVID MERCER

*

Ramsay took on Mercer (1928–80) in 1960 after an acquaintance asked her to read a play of his as a favour. He was scraping a living as a teacher.

13 January 1961

Dear David,

We hope you are going to think this letter a compliment, though your Bank Manager probably won't appreciate it!

The point is this: we have so far been earning money for you and not taking commission or deferring it, and we have paid for a set of scripts of THE BURIED MAN.

Now it seems to me that we must now consider you a professional writer and this means you will have to pay your agent 10%.

Love to you both,

My dear David,

You cannot expect an actor to bring something of himself to your play, anything he can bring is a mere bonus. Remember, your "Buried Man" is a passive man, things happen to him, he does not make anything happen. This is the whole problem of your bloody play. However, you are obviously learning a tremendous amount and you will be surprised how patient provincial audiences are. They are quite used to dead actors.

I read the new play [The Governor's Lady]. I must join Mr. [*David*] Jones in not being really crazy about it. I find great difficulty in differentiating between your hero and the gorilla. Your hero is pretty unattractive and so heavy-footed. Actually, what I am trying to say is that the comedy does not come off because it's too heavy. You were quite right not to show me beforehand because I would have asked you to re-write half a dozen scenes.

I think the play could have been very good but you are going to have to learn to use a lighter touch and not only write a play but re-write it. My only worry is that this is not going to extend your reputation and any play you write now should do this.

Well, get through this year somehow, but I beg you to see that you do only first-class work in 1963. Let us have a very serious talk about this and let's make some kind of plan. Discuss and be quite sure before you start any play that it's the right theme and play and that you know where you are going. The trouble about this year is that like your hero in "The Buried Man", things are happening to you and you are not making things happen.

In your letter you asked me to write you a loving note! I don't think this is the letter you asked for but I will try and be more loving next time.

Affectionately,

My dear David,

Why do disasters make so much better reading than the happy spells? Have you not considered the fact that you are still very adolescent as far as women are concerned. You still have these absurd romantic illusions.

After all, they are just a bit of cunt and you should keep your friendships and emotions separate from your sexual desires. However, we wouldn't get such good stage plays from you, and I shall expect to see a manuscript entitled LA BAIE DOREE interpreting some of the adventures you write of in your letters.

I don't quite understand why you need a complete suite with kitchen and bathroom upstairs when you have a complete suite downstairs. After all, your lady of the moment could have her own bedroom and the use of the bath. She doesn't have to intrude into your study. However, I seem to remember that you have only one bedroom on the lower floor so I can understand your wanting another. I trust that along with the shower will go a bidet.

I think there was a certain amount of publicity on Mercer, but the occasion was chiefly used for the convenience of Pinter, who was interviewed in depth on LATE NIGHT LINE UP only I couldn't be bothered to watch.

I am so tired of your friend Joan Bakewell now disporting herself like some film starlet. Last night I switched on to see Patricia Neale but all the camera angles and bridling were done by Mrs Bakewell, who seems to think that she's an object of beauty and no longer bothers to ask the right questions and listen to the answers. Pinter also chatted on radio and generally it was a pretty good publicity week for him. I would rather like to have an excellent few days for Mercer and we must arrange this!

For God's sake don't do any more hell-raising with those gendarmes.

Looking forward to seeing you on your return.

Love,

Alan Bridges directed four Mercer plays on television.

28 November 1969

Dear Alan,

Of course you love your work before weighing any advantages to yourself from it. This is evident by what you do – only those who work <u>for the work itself</u> can show results such as yours.

From my point of view, I have no interest in my work as such at all, (if we are talking about my firm), nor have I any interest in either the theatre or the cinema, or TV <u>as such</u>. To me the only interest is in <u>life</u>, and these arts, (stage cinema etc.), like painting and all the rest, are <u>reflections</u> of life, and should enhance and enrich life, but are nothing at all in themselves, except that creative people (which I am not), have got to forget that they are operating reflections. But none of us should love the reflections without living the actuality more. Most people I know in this business, seem to love the theatre as such. I have no religion, but I imagine that the phrase about worshipping graven images could apply here!

You must think me a prize bitch, the way I talk about people. The point is, that if they can take it, I'll give it to them direct, but no "truth" about anyone is said with hate. It's just necessary to know their weaknesses and their strength, I'd know all about the people you are to work with, because the success of any venture is the sum total of all the talents, weaknesses and strength of the people concerned.

Love,

Mercer wrote Ramsay from Haifa where he was staying with Dafna, his third wife, whom he had married in 1974. They settled in Israel and Mercer died there.

19 July 1976

My Dear Mercer,

Just received your July 14 letter and rush to answer it.

You couldn't live in Israel and write for the theatre, David. You could only live there if the theatre really doesn't matter to you.

It's not missing interviews with these top Directors which is the main problem. It's keeping out of touch with the collective subconscious of England.

Love,

JOHN MORTIMER

John Holmstrom showed Ramsay the first play by Mortimer (1923–2009) in 1957 and she agreed to represent him. He stayed until her death. Michael Elliott directed Mortimer's Two Stars for Comfort *in 1962, with Trevor Howard as Sam Turner.*

23 March 1962

Dear Michael,

Yes, I fully agree with you regarding Trevor Howard – but the whole problem of "SAM" is the crux of the matter, isn't it? By this I mean he hasn't any inner being, or at least Mortimer has never asked himself – 'how do I stand regarding Sam, what is my attitude to him, what is the attitude of the audience to be to him?' Every man has a philosophy, and a morality, even if he doesn't know it – but what exactly is Sam's? We know a hell of a lot about him, but far less than we know about a man we met briefly for a few minutes. For instance, I suppose I could write a long article on what I believe you to be, and it would contain none of the "small change" of life – by that I mean it wouldn't even mention that you happen to be married, but it would, I think, be recognisably <u>you</u>. I could do the same for Mortimer. The trouble with SAM is that there is too much periphery and not sufficient indication of what he IS. This is what makes it so tremendously hard for Trevor to play him. Yes, he's unsympathetic, but so is IAGO, but the latter is riveting, because one sees the movement of his mind. We should see more of the movement of SAM'S.

This is, actually, Mortimer's big failing to my mind. He himself hasn't got a true philosophy and wouldn't know, if you asked him, where he <u>stands</u>. In the old days it didn't matter in the theatre, because we were only interested in surface, but now we want to try and see how people tick – it's not <u>quite</u> possible at the moment to say how SAM ticks – he <u>can't</u> be as empty as he seems, surely?

137

Forgive me for using such exaggerated words – don't think for a moment I expect this to be any part of the criticism of the play, which will be a big success. It's just that the only thing I'm really interested in is <u>what drives a man</u>, and it's discernible in quite a short time in real life.

You might say that this was also the case in THE WRONG SIDE OF THE PARK. This is too true. But John was writing about an idle, selfish, empty woman, who could only live through other people, and oddly enough one recognised this woman. Sam tends to be more nebulous – there is his charm, his sex instincts, his weakness, his kindness but this isn't all.

Mortimer has far far more himself – much of it quite ugly – (but then we are all of us <u>everything</u>, and this isn't meant as a criticism, merely as a recognition of our goodness and badness). Mortimer's big weakness is a passion for success and the trappings of success, and the awful part of it is that success, when indulged in, saps people's character, and drains their true potential talent away – the people who love successful people exploit them, take them up, throw them away, and sometimes only a shell is left.

Mortimer has a rare and touching talent, a remarkable sense of atmosphere, deep sympathy and a moving plaintive voice – he could be a superb artist, not merely a successful one, and it's this which makes me sad. If only he could find happiness and enrichment in his own talent, and the exercise of such talent….the shoddy prizes are fun to receive, but are valueless.

One day, will you tell me exactly what the theme of this play is? What should we feel about Sam? Regret, sympathy, a slight kinship? Yes, but he hasn't really shown us his true self, and I find this terribly unsatisfactory, because I have the feel that people go to the theatre for <u>something</u> – solace, help, understanding, and so on, and it's the duty of the playwright to comfort and help them and <u>nourish them</u>.

Of course you agree with all this; I don't know why I'm writing it really. Perhaps regret that I can't say it to Mortimer himself!

How lucky we all are to have you. You are the only director I feel <u>confident</u> about, wholly.

PETER NICHOLS

*

Nichols (1927–) joined Ramsay in 1959 with three television plays to his name. Over the next three decades, he left and returned again a couple of times.

12 September 1977

Dear Peter,

Thanks for your long and interesting letter to me. I don't at all agree about people, their character and what they are. I am aware that the theatre is a fairly fifth-rate, shitty place and we are probably all tarred with being in the theatre. However, when you say that "we are what we do", I simply don't believe it. I think that people have tremendous private reserves. I have just read a play about the Bounty and the Bounty collapse happened because of the characters under pressure. The first big crisis was due to the carpenter, who was a brilliant carpenter but was not prepared to do anything else that was not carpentry of some sort, even though he'd been told that everyone would have to work as a team and be prepared to do each other's work. Bligh certainly did everyone's work whenever he could. But, had it not been for the pressure of isolation and the lack of food and the general privation, this carpenter's character would never have emerged. I don't think it would have emerged on shore.

I don't agree with your bleak sense that there is "not as much to know about people as they'd like you to believe." I think the people who pose as mysterious possibly <u>have</u> nothing to be mysterious about. That people don't talk about their private lives, their politics or their religion doesn't mean that they are only what they are at work. I am of the opposite opinion, and I believe that nine-tenths of what people are is hidden, and I wouldn't wish to go on living if I thought they should be judged on the natural façade they put on during working hours.

From my own point of view, I made a decision when I first became an agent that I would in no way intrude on any of the authors we represented. Because they were our clients, I certainly didn't claim their friendship, and it would be entirely impertinent to do so. A few have become friends with some to a limited extent, but I don't think one should mix business and friendship, except in rare circumstances.

Love,

Nichols had left Ramsay to join another agent, Michael Imison, but did return.

13 May 1981 [handwritten]

Dear Peter,

It was nice of you to think of returning, but Michael Imison isn't likely to let you go, but <u>at least</u> it's put a squib up his arse, to your advantage.

Your letter <u>amazes</u> me in its pessimism. This time last year you had just only written "Garden" [Born in the Gardens] – it went on at Bristol and transferred to <u>excellent</u> notices and it's done better than almost any W.E. play…<u>Of course</u> the W.E. isn't dead but every time any of us say so, we inflict a wound.

M. I. has inherited one of the best known, most successful authors in the English speaking world – <u>when are you going to enjoy</u> your position and reputation? It's <u>perverse</u> to punish yourself for your success (because that is what you are doing).

"Emigrate? Write novels, contemplate your navel?" No – in ten years you'll have written at least five more plays which will keep your position going, until you no longer have any inclination to continue writing, and then the subsidiary rights will keep you in plush.

Success is a <u>rum</u> thing. It doesn't bring happiness or security. Maybe it's a way to <u>make you go on</u>, and that suffering is good for writing. But <u>IS</u> it? You have such a <u>joyous</u> talent; it never deserts you. You are at the prime of your career and I <u>refuse</u> to be sorry for you, you lucky bugger.

Love,

Dear Hare,

I'm writing to you because my mind wandered to P. Nichols, who is such a superb character for a play…

For instance, I think I told you how, when he was living back-to-back to Michael Frayn, he copied his suits, his spectacles, his mannerisms, his 'wit'. In the end Frayn had to move to another neighbourhood. Nobody else seemed to notice this, but one day I said to Frayn, "I was interested in seeing you being eaten alive by Nichols", and he burst out laughing. (If you remember, for a short time Osborne became Chekhov – spectacles, beard and all!)

But dwelling on Nichols, I began to consider his <u>vulgarity</u> and his ambitions. When he moved to London (to beat Stoppard at his own game), he went to any and every cocktail party, and moved in on all the celebrities. Then he asked them for their telephone numbers and invited them round – they had to reciprocate and that is how he is featured in the "Tatler" this month. Finally, he now knows pretty well <u>every</u> fashionable name in the West End and his climb became <u>immediate</u>. No doubt newspaper men have GOT to do this, but <u>writers</u>?

Love,

JOE ORTON

*

On the advice of BBC radio producer John Tydeman, Orton (1933–67) showed Ramsay Entertaining Mr Sloane *and she agreed to represent him.*

Dear Harold [*Hobson*, Sunday Times *critic*],

I do hope you won't be too busy next week, as I so much want you to see the little play at the Arts called ENTERTAINING MR. SLOANE.

This play came to me in January and I thought it extremely talented and asked to meet the author. A young man called and I was much struck with him. I frankly told him that I was uncertain about the advisability of selling this play in case the critics might label it "Pinterish". He replied that I must do anything I wished and that he could easily manage if I didn't sell it, because he was living on £3. 10. 0d p.w. National Assistance, and had been doing so "ever since he came out". He then went on to tell me that he had been six months in Wormwood Scrubs for a series of minor thefts and that it had been remarkably good for him. When I asked if he intended going back to crime, he said certainly not, if it was possible to earn his living in any other way.

Finally, I decided to get this play done quickly at the Arts. Peter Wood was dying to direct it but Wood can never commit himself to any date, so we decided to get a more modest Director. In the meantime, I've been trying to help the author with money, but he firmly and tactfully says it's quite unnecessary and that he "can manage". I even offered him a TV set as a present, but he said he was quite all right without one!

I am much struck with a young man who doesn't want to exploit people, who is prepared to live on £3. 10. 0d p.w., who doesn't whine, or tell a hard luck tale.

I'm therefore particularly keen that his play should have a proper showing. I don't know what you will think of it. I hope you will like it. My main desire is for Joe to have a chance.

Best regards,

Yours,

Orton's Loot *was first produced on a pre-London tour by Michael Codron and Donald Albery.*

10 February 1965

Dear Michael,

I've got a fearful cold, so this letter may be a bit fuzzy.

I thought the Tuesday performance of the play at Brighton very much slicker and more professional, and this play is already better than SLOANE was at any time – it's a better play.

But though it was smoother and altogether funnier, it could now be called a "farce", because it has become more conventional, and is beginning, very slightly, to lose Joe's personal and unique voice.

I am writing now, quickly begging you not to turn it into a John Chapman play, and to remember all the time exactly what play you bought in the first place, and not find yourself with another, perhaps very popular, but nearer to a Whitehall farce than an Orton play.

I was a bit alarmed to hear that you were going to "prepare" Kenneth [*Williams*]'s remark about being from the Water Board. But surely the original prologue did exactly this, and spoiled Kenneth's entrance? I thought preparing things went out in the plays of the '30s, when two small parts "talked about" the leading characters in order to "prepare" an audience.

The whole essence of a Joe Orton talent is the surprise, the dottiness and inconsequence of most of the remarks. If everything is going to be "prepared" we get an old fashioned, certain number-two tour laugh – no surprise, no modern voice, just a regular old fashioned farce approach.

I am not saying you won't get a success by explaining everything and making everything <u>logical</u> – but Orton isn't logical, he is perverse and surprising, and if you make him logical you will destroy his voice.

<u>Of course</u>, you have not done this yet – though the laugh about the mummy is damn near it. Sure, it's a laugh, but a provincial laugh, which could have come from any farce at Whitehall. I beg you to remember the <u>kind</u> of play you bought, and have the courage not to play safe and destroy the talent of the author.

God knows, too many people have been having their say. Binkie is largely to blame for going on about <u>who</u> Kenneth's character was, and where he came from. The play was spoiled on Monday at Cambridge by a Prologue which told us that Kenneth was a detective. We only need a few banana skins, and we would get even more laughs.

Please try and preserve Joe's voice, and don't play safe and explain everything. If we do explain everything we shall have a kind of BOEING-BOEING success, which is nice for the pocket, but I'd rather never sell another author to a Management who was prepared to iron out all his originality and wit.

So – this letter is wildly exaggerated, but a warning not to <u>explain</u> everything – if you do, you make Joe join forces with such plays as BREATH OF SPRING and THE DIPLOMATIC BAGGAGE, both successful, but who gets prestige from plays of this sort.

Lots of luck, and keep up the passion you are showing about getting this play a <u>success</u>.

Love,

9 March 1965

Dear Michael,

Your letter of 6 March, charming as it is, seems to have been written from some other country from the one I am inhabiting, so far from my own feelings does your interpretation of them present!

I've written two letters about the play, only. I have, in each letter, tried to express an intuitive and instinctive fear.

I've been selling you plays for years, and I <u>always</u> present you with my fears, as I want any play you do of ours to make you money and make your reputation. Suddenly, however, I appear to be a kind of interloper, not en rapport with the "in" people. I'm treated to a disgusting letter from Joe and extraordinary behaviour from you. But I'm "outside" in exactly the same way as your audience is "outside" and the critics are "outside". I have the feeling that I'd be the most popular girl in the class provided I just said "wonderful" all the time.

I'm NOT a highbrow. Don't forget I actually sent BOEING-BOEING to Jack Minster. You can hardly go lower-brow than <u>that</u>. I fell in love, of all things, with <u>Dr. Finlay</u>['s Casebook] when it first came out. So, I'm not talking as an avant-garde person, who wants everything enigmatic and inaccessible.

I wrote those two letters because I was urged to do so by my subconscious, which registered some fears that the play might be becoming a bit banal and "ordinary" – and therefore get jibes regarding being like the Aunt Edna author [*Rattigan*].

But <u>if it's funny</u>, it's never banal or "ordinary" – I just wanted to beg you to try and lean over backwards in not allowing the play to flatten out too much.

It seems to me that the lesson I must learn from this, is that if I am to continue in the theatre, I must become like every other agent – flattering and hypocritical and say it's an absolutely brilliant play and a brilliant production and that our bloody critics are absolutely out of touch, and that everything is quite <u>wonderful</u>. This is the way Peter Bridge runs his firm. Everything is <u>always</u> wonderful, and the box-office <u>always</u> lies. Full marks for perseverance.

Clearly I'm out of step with you all and had better shut up, since everything I say seems to be judged as a vitriolic attack on what is going on.

You'll be happy to hear that Lindsay [*Anderson*], Tony Page, Devine, Ann [*Jellicoe*], and I have been asked to appear in a play together, and I must say I'm tempted to view the theatre from behind the protective barrier of the footlights. I'm even considering accepting an invitation to talk on A.R. TV [*Associated Rediffusion*] about the theatre – this can give you some idea of how much I am detesting my metier at the moment, and how little I value it.

Yours,

Ramsay believed the production, directed by Peter Wood, was a disaster and urged its cancellation. Orton talked of leaving her, and she and Codron reached the lowest point in their long relationship. Loot *closed in March 1965 before coming into the West End but both Orton and Ramsay believed in the play and wanted to revive it.*

My dear Joe,

It's very early Tuesday morning, and I can't sleep because of one of those long smoky drinky evenings with Binkie, when he plots away trying to manipulate the theatre. They always amuse and interest me, but don't finally give one anything but a bad night's sleep. He's trying to manoeuvre me to arrange that one of our authors should join him and Fred Zinnemann in a film trio, and I just can't be sure if it's to the advantage of the author! Am I being "used" to persuade him to do something not to his final advantage? My views are that freedom is everything, and that this is the one thing "success" brings an author. Also an author <u>needs</u> no tight set up of this sort, whereas a non-creative person like a Director and a Manager would obviously find it useful to have an exclusive link with an author...

Oscar [*Lewenstein*] has jaundice and is away. I have the feeling that the Court and Oscar want to do RUFFIAN [on the Stair] first, as a first step to LOOT. [John] Dexter phoned for a copy a few days ago, so obviously he is one of the most likely to do the play – as you know he straddles both the Court and the National, and is a brilliant director and himself a cold, calculating man. I can't tell you how pleased I am that LOOT production was withdrawn, as it was a <u>confection</u> and tricky. I can't help being touched by Wood, however, who is so emotional and absurd really, and whom I found treatling [*sic*] like a wounded child during the [The Prime of Miss Jean] BRODIE horrors of rehearsal. He kept moaning to me "You're <u>so</u> <u>calm</u>"!!! And of course I was, as the author was behaving like a monster and one gets a kind of grim pleasure because one is detached and anyway I knew we would have a success with the production in spite of the hell we were going through. Wood is now recovering in Greece – a good idea. He spoke with admiration of you and bears no grudge whatsoever.

Michael is busy with his two trivial comedies. Did I tell you I had to pay his share of a commission on a play he instigated with Francis King? I offered to "go" one fifth, but when the play was delivered Michael didn't like it (nor did I) and refused to honour the contract. I told him that I would therefore HAVE to pay since a bargain was a bargain, and to my astonishment he let me do it, though he must have realised that at least ONE ally of his wouldn't really trust him in future. This is the vice of <u>meanness</u> which can destroy a man and a career.

I went to the Court on Sunday to see Christopher Hampton's play WHEN DID YOU LAST SEE MY MOTHER? which we represent. It's a young man's play, and he doesn't yet know much about people, but I liked it when he asked me to look after him and I sent it to the Court. I wish you had been there to see how well the Court do plays of this sort. The play won't go further, I don't think; and anyway the writer is still at Oxford and only in his second year. I'd like your opinion on him.

Nothing "grand" is happening except there is this big important George Devine night at the National. Tickets cost about 10 guineas each, and though I was devoted to George, and I've supported his fund (I give my commission I earn at the Court to it) I wasn't going to go. Imagine my horror, when <u>Binkie</u> invited me. He is on the Award Scheme committee with Olivier, and I'm stuck with this party. They are doing snips of all the plays performed at the Court – the Knack and that kind of thing. Most unnourishing, as an evening, but everyone will be in their diamonds and tiaras. I was invited by Mrs Sieff to a cocktail party two weeks ago to talk about the Award and this "do" (she is a Marks and Spencer). It was fairly grotesque, with Lady Redgrave telling me that she missed George more and more each day, and oddly enough I miss the old boy too, but because he was so wry and cynical and grimly amused. In return I'm inviting Binkie to lunch to meet Alan Brien, because Binkie hates Brien because he gives H.M. Tennent bad notices. I foresee a somewhat rough lunch, as Binkie says his new line is "attack", whatever he thinks that means.

I hope you're not frantic about LOOT. My feelings are these: it is certain to go on, but I want to have the best possible production, either at the Court or wherever (the National?) and if we have to wait a month or three months, it doesn't matter, because this time we must succeed with it – no muffing.

Please give regards to Ken [*Halliwell*]. I like to think of you both having this life in Marrakesh and enjoying it. I hope it may prove fruitful. I urge ONE of you, at least, to start a journal, a la Gide; I'm sure it would be a good idea and the publishers would snap at it. I suggest Faber and Faber for a book. I've become friends with Charles Monteith who has just presented me with a lovely Greek cookbook. He's always open for a commission. Why not talk this over with Ken, who has real writing talent, but finds stage plots difficult.

Love,

as ever,

A Manchester production of Loot *in April 1966 was followed by a London production in September that transferred from its fringe venue to the West End and won Orton the Evening Standard Best Play Award. He took Ramsay to the award ceremony and dedicated the published text to her. He was murdered in August 1967 by his partner Kenneth Halliwell.*

15 August 1967

Dear Miss Lee [*Evans Plays*],

How very kind of you to write such a kind letter on the 14 August regarding Joe Orton's tragic death.

I think it would be quite wrong to have a tribute included in your edition of LOOT. Your edition will be sold for many years to come on the merit of the play. We hope that the events of his private life will be forgotten as soon as possible. As you know, we are in a profession called the "entertainment business" and I think that the private tragedies of the authors shouldn't emerge in the volumes of their plays distributed for the rehearsals of the play. In London the audience is still laughing at LOOT and isn't embarrassed. I feel that the actors receiving any script of the text with a memorium [*sic*] might be reluctant to do the play.

Sincerely,

3 November 1967

Dear Harold [*Hobson,* Sunday Times *critic*],

I have now got you a copy of the Orton diary for your private reading. It turns out to be 102 foolscap pages of one and a half spaced typing.

I think you will be immeasurably bored and sad because you will possibly feel, as I do, that for our tastes this would be most boring way of spending a holiday one could possibly contrive.

I have been thinking more about my antipathy towards WISE CHILD [*by Simon Gray*], which I haven't yet seen. I suppose that while you were so right in saying that no subject is unsuitable for the theatre, a boulevard piece on a rather serious "deviation" subject is not the same thing as this kind of thing done by a great man like Genet. Isn't it perhaps a matter of talent rather than of subject? To bring this sad aspect of human relationships into a well-made little play and then get it performed by one of our great leading actors [*Alec Guinness*] is above all the most serious waste of time, spirit and talent. So, when we say something of this sort is corrupting, it is corrupting our tastes and reducing our standards.

If you would like to talk to me after you have read the diary please tell me, and perhaps I can give you lunch at your favourite restaurant.

Warm regards,

10 January 1968

Dear Saint [*Subber, US producer*]

The real trouble is that every career goes on <u>too long</u>, and that after 30 everything repeats itself – it's just the names which are different. Somehow or other one has to renew oneself daily and not just wait for the seven- year change of cells. Our bloody metier destroys the inner life and one has no retreat from outside attack.

Our theatre in England is probably worse off than yours, because you still have a few years to squeeze the juices of the avant-garde. We have had this for ten years now and there's nothing more in that line for us.

I was very interested in your mention of Capote. Of course I have thought about him in conjunction with Joe. But the diary is only one tiny piece of evidence, and the rest of his life too is chock full of interest. I lunched with Charles Monteith of Faber on Monday, because Faber want to commission a writer to write a book on Joe, and have suggested John Bowen. This choice is an interesting one for reasons I won't bore you with. I haven't spoken to John as Faber want to approach him.

Monteith met Joe and Ken Halliwell when the two of them were sharing a tiny room in Hampstead in the early '60s, living on the remains of the money left to Ken when his parents committed suicide. They met when Joe, a young country-boy, joined the Royal College of Dramatic Art at the age of 17. He was simple, in love with the theatre and absolutely naïve. Halliwell was several years older, brought up in the city and with a strong exhibitionist streak. He must have dominated and impressed the youthful Joe, and I found a laconic note in an early diary that within a week Joe had moved into Ken's room.

Obviously they were both terrible actors, and at some stage decided to become great writers. They staked what remained of Ken's inheritance in keeping them while they wrote their chefs-d'oeuvre. These novels in which they collaborated were sent to Charles Monteith who turned them down, but was fascinated by the pair. He tells me that they had no friends of any sort, and lived entirely alone, spinning out their money. They got up as soon as it was light and went to bed when it became dark in order to save electricity. They used to spend the afternoons reading aloud to each other; Monteith remembers the time they were reading Gibbon, for instance. Then they ran out of money and worked at Cadbury's chocolate factory part-time, so that they had time for writing. The last note Monteith got was that Joe had decided to write plays alone.

In the Tangier Diary it was clear that Joe and Ken dedicated their holiday to sex (young Arab boys) and hashish. Ken baked a hashish cake each day. Ken was obviously trying to tell Joe what to do – warning him about excess and generally nagging. Joe was impatient and irritated. At one stage there was a dress-rehearsal for death, because Ken began hitting Joe on the head in rage (later at the flat he killed him by hammering him on the head while he lay asleep).

When they returned to London from Tangier Ken was obviously anxious that Joe didn't create some kind of scandal by his sexual indiscretions (there were sorties to gents lavatories and pick-ups of various sorts). In addition Ken must have come to the end of accepting that Joe was a desired success and nobody cared about <u>him</u>, except as Joe's friend. He had a bad patch of depression. His stupid doctor didn't realise it was serious. So he battered Joe to death and swallowed a handful of what Joe called in his Diary "Ken's suicide pills". I had to go to the flat shortly after the murder and it was a sight I'll not easily forget. On the other hand, Ken, laid out was like a magnificent Roman Emperor – enormously impressive in death.

Two separate inquests and two separate funerals had to be arranged, and I went to both. Ken had not seen any of his family for 17 years. There were two sisters and one brother from his mother's side. Respectable "superior" and composed. We protected them from the Press.

Both were cremated in different parts of London – Ken first – but I arranged that Ken's ashes were taken to Golders Green Cemetery and scattered with Joe's. This was a secret arrangement and the Press didn't hear. I doubt if anyone knew except the families and the respective undertakers. Ken's service was conducted by a clergyman at Enfield in the chapel – hymns and an organ featured. Joe had no funeral service. One of the Beatles songs was played on a tape (Joe's favourite) and short poems read respectively by Donald Pleasance and Harold Pinter. A badly stage-managed affair with gaps before the tape started and a gap before the poems. It was "organised" by Peter Willes, the head of Drama at Rediffusion TV who said he specialised in funerals, and who doted on Joe. I hadn't the heart to tell him later that funerals were not his speciality. Nobody came to Ken's funeral at all, and only the cast of LOOT, our firm and Joe's family went to his. The Press were, of course, seething round but got everything wrong.

Joe's family (his father is blind and earns his living as a gardener in Leicester) is now headed by Joe's younger brother [*Douglas*], who is a plumber. He is extremely poised and practical. When I went with him to the undertaker to arrange the funeral he said that flowers were ridiculous, unnecessary and a needless expense. He added that Joe's mother had recently died and Joe certainly didn't send HER flowers!

Warmest regards,

Lewenstein-Delfont Productions and H.M. Tennent produced Orton's What the Butler Saw. *It opened on a pre-London tour.*

17 February 1969

Dear Oscar [*Lewenstein*],

At your request and at Binkie's request, I saw WHAT THE BUTLER SAW on Saturday night, and I don't feel awfully happy about writing this letter, but it would be silly of me to conceal my anxiety.

To my mind the play is not nearly as good as it was at the opening in Cambridge. It has all tended to become very rigid. Though the machinery of the play has now become fluid, and the actual physical situations are now excellent, the evening, particularly Act One, is not fun.

I think there is far too much mouthing of the text. Joe's style can now surely be left to look after itself, and a little more speed, ease and enjoyment could creep in. There is no feeling of enjoyment or zest or expansion, and I think the actors have all become tense, and aren't enjoying or expanding or feeling any zest in their parts whatsoever, most particularly Sir Ralph.

When the play closes, I think he will admit that he wished he had never been persuaded to do the part. He seemed to be forcing himself to go through it all.

The Actors need encouraging to relax, to play things with more ease, not simply recite the words as if they were Holy Writ. Joe didn't put such a special value on his prose. It happens to be very good indeed, but quite a lot of writers write very good prose, but actors aren't asked to mouth and grimace the words, the way poor Joe's work is being mouthed and grimaced.

The audience wasn't bad, and gave it a big hand. Dickie Eastham said to me in the interval, "Is this the play that Joe didn't finish!?", and I saw his point. The play begins stiffly and seems to be half frozen, and perhaps that gives it an unfinished look.

I'm sorry to burden you with this note on your return from New York. If you wish to ignore this letter, please do so.

Love,

Dear John Lahr [*US critic*],

I look forward to seeing you in July, but probably quite naturally, feel disturbed about your writing a book on Orton. Disturbed because of Kenneth Halliwell, who killed him.

Joe was a small-town country boy, who met Kenneth in his first week at RADA, and Kenneth was a rather more sophisticated townee, about ten years older than Joe, with these obsessions about violence, death, and all the paraphernalia that appears every Sunday in the News of the World. Joe's very early diaries are so simple and so naïve, that one realises that if he had not met Kenneth, he would have never become the writer he is now.

Kenneth's family left him a little bit of money, which subsidised the two of them in a small room, and all day they read classics aloud to one another, and it was during that time that they studied Firbank and Wilde in such detail. Also, during that time, they wrote very bad novels together, and sent them to Faber and Faber, who didn't want to publish them, but were interested enough to go and have tea with them one day.

When they began running out of money, they used to work in the day-time and earn their living at night in an ice-cream factory in order to save electric light. When Joe sent me SLOANE, he always spoke of the play as 'we', and after he'd visited me the first time, he always brought Kenneth with him afterwards, and Kenneth always attended rehearsals. I had a very strong impression that they worked on this together, but had decided not to use both their names where plays were concerned. As time passed, Joe's extraordinary charm captured everyone, whereas Kenneth's rather brittle, sharp manner didn't. Certainly Kenneth improved when he began wearing a wig. He was quite bald, and was very ashamed of his baldness, and kept his hat on everywhere, including in the theatre. The first money Joe earned was spent on a couple of wigs for Kenneth, and he chose a style with a rather endearing forelock. I think that by looking at himself in the mirror and seeing someone rather charming and sincere, it actually altered his personality, and he became rather charming and sincere, so that indeed I quite forgot my first alarmed reaction to his personality.

I think their two or three visits to Tangiers were very disastrous, because they went in for pot-eating to excess, but the diary I have got, which covers three months in Marrakesh hardly mentions the theatre at all. Joe seemed very detached from the theatre altogether, and not particularly ambitious, except to write very well, and during the last six months, he didn't even seem to want to write.

Though a lot of people tried to make life pleasant for Kenneth, he was desperately aware of the fact that Joe was a success and liked, and he was a failure and not liked. At a party given by someone after a television play of Joe's a Producer turned to Kenneth and said "what are you doing here, you're not wanted, you're nobody". I think this was the final blow to Kenneth, who was already fairly deranged from his months in Morocco, and while Joe was visiting his parents, he became morbid, and the day Joe returned, he obviously felt he didn't want to go on living, and while Joe was asleep he took a hammer and beat out his brains. Immediately after that he took a whole bottle of pills. He was discovered on the floor naked and dead, and at the autopsy it was discovered that he had died before Joe, because Joe was still warm under the bed-clothes.

This was very important, because both of them had left a will leaving everything to each other, and we were a little worried that Kenneth's family (which he'd not seen for twenty-five years), might claim all Joe's Estate, and leave Joe's impecunious little family without anything. Fortunately, by British law, a murderer's family cannot benefit from the murderer's victim, so we were okay on both counts.

I'm not being sentimental when I say that Joe wouldn't in the least mind being killed by Kenneth. He was very casual about life, and he didn't get a great kick out of success, which he took with a wry smile. He and Kenneth had shared so much together, years of struggle to educate themselves, six months in prison and the time after prison before Joe showed me SLOANE.

SLOANE was put on five or six weeks after he first sent it to the office, and in a way, it became stupidly easy for Joe after that. I'd have to ask Douglas, Joe's brother if you can read his Moroccan diary. It's very boring on the whole, but rather spectacularly frank about sex. If you are serious about writing a book about Joe, you had better meet Joe's brother, who is very like Joe. He is a plumber and lives in Leicester.

Sincerely yours,

Dear John [*Lahr*],

I am deeply upset by these articles giving the impression that Management, stars and Directors are either without talent or deliberately seeking success [*in the US*] at the cost of the play [What the Butler Saw], and that I am frivolously allowing Joe's play to be bowdlerised. The production in London was a failure, and an astute critic over here could perhaps have said that it might have been due to certain omissions, because Richardson wasn't prepared to say some of the lines or include some of the dialogue, so that neither London nor New York has seen exactly what Joe wrote.

I think it's almost impossible that a play by a dead author which he didn't revise and which he didn't discuss with any Director or anyone else since he died a few days after finishing it can be treated as if nothing whatever can be touched in it. Apart from actors' changes in London it was treated like the Gospel (though, of course, the Gospel is constantly bowdlerised and survives so that this is a very inept comparison). Joe died before he had even signed the Contract – the text came out of his drawer when he returned from Marrakesh, and quite apart from adding one link scene he left the revisions for rehearsals. He used to revise heavily at rehearsals for both stage and TV, and you could talk to any Director who directed Joe's plays and you will be amazed how easy he was and how well prepared he was to have matters pointed out to him. I absolutely agree that the final scene should have been staged and rehearsed in New York, and if it hadn't worked at the previews then there would have been a valid reason for considering its omission. There have been many failures of the play in Germany vis a vis this last scene, and though they have soldiered on, the play isn't getting many more bookings in Germany, though I am sure it has nothing to do with this last scene, which needs properly preparing for. If a scene doesn't work one must look at the previous scenes to see how one leads into the difficult scene. Joe Hardy is a comedy Director and stressed the comedy, just as many people used to play Chekhov as a tragedy and have now gone the opposite way and decided to play him almost as a farce. This hasn't hurt Chekhov whose play remains, and nor will it hurt Orton, whose play remains, and there could be very different interpretations of all his plays.

John, dear, you exercise power every time you stand in public in judgement as an expert on Orton. Please use it wisely and carefully and with some feeling of compassion.

All Joe's plays are difficult. All have failed financially, and, apart from LOOT, critically. Joe always allowed Directors to have freedom. We simply can't take a totally academic and righteous stand. I seriously suggest that you should direct BUTLER yourself, and you will see that every production has to have emphasis on different aspects, and this applies to every play ever written. Bergman has left out 15 pages of the 45 pages of HEDDA GABLER for the National production. We all do THE BEAUX' STRATAGEM without the sub-plot, and probably only academics know there is a sub-plot.

I am simply asking for a degree of kindness and understanding towards the people who have been trying to do Orton, because this is what he would have given them had he been here himself, and you are going to speak for him in the near future, so I do call to your attention his extraordinary generous attitude towards the people he worked with. He remained devoted to Kenneth Williams and Peter Wood, even though they had "destroyed" the original LOOT – that shows you the kind of boy he was.

Love,

10 June 1975

Dear Jill [*Bennett*],

I always avoid any party so I didn't join you for drinks after the first night, and I might have some things to say about the part and play [Loot] to you, but these should wait until the play is over!

I thought the play was tremendously interesting. I did not realise that Fay could be played vulnerable. Joe was so hard himself and so amoral that he would have liked to see it played other than as a kind of minor Myra Hindley.

Love,

Ramsay corresponded with her solicitor Laurence Harbottle about John Lahr's forthcoming Orton biography.

16 September 1977

Dear Laurence,

We have got to go through with it now. We can't interfere, and to get you to read the manuscript would cause such hysteria from Lahr, who imagines that there is some ulterior motive for my concern about the diary, i.e. perhaps he thinks I am jealous of him or I want power over Joe – in fact, all the things inside himself he is transferring to me.

If I were jealous of writers, it would certainly not be someone like Lahr, since we have so many creative writers here of whom I could be jealous, were I such a person. Nor do I have any particular feeling for Joe – I liked him as a person and I liked his plays a great deal. I did not think he was a genius.

Love,

The biography appeared in 1978 called Prick Up Your Ears, *a title Ramsay had suggested to Orton he use for his play* Funeral Games.

5 October 1978

Dear John Lahr,

We trusted you, and therefore in 1970 I gave you all my papers, quotations, Joe's diaries, photos, and asked Douglas, as Administrator of the Estate, to do all in his power to help you write a book on Joe. You took everything away, and nobody was allowed access or information from that day to this.

Since that time you have refused to sign any Contract which might have given minimum copyright protection and control of Joe's own copyrighted work to the Estate. But last year when Penguin finally had to have some authority to proceed with publication, I urged Douglas to give you some authority, and he signed that bit of paper in Harbottle's office.

When the proofs were ready, you sent them to Douglas, telling him not to show them to me. He sent them to me at once, with your message. I threw them on a shelf unread, and posted them back to him when he asked for them.

You sent me via your Publisher a copy of the printed work. I put it aside unopened. Did you think I would <u>read</u> it?

You have used me as far as I was useful, and then you deliberately told people not to get in touch with me, and you have set up articles, quotes and film rights in your book which included copyrighted material yourself.

You never knew Joe. He was honourable and loyal. He would have been disappointed in your behaviour.

I do not regret giving you access to all the material, because you are a very talented writer. I feel only disillusion.

Yours sincerely,

4 November 1980

Dear John,

Regarding casting, and Jeanne Moreau, the part [*in the film* Prick Up Your Ears *based on Lahr's biography*] would have to be a bit more interesting for her to take it. It needs to be more eccentric in any case, don't you think? In any case, it's not at all like me, and of course, I am not interested in my own depiction, simply that it should be a really good part in a film.

Best regards,

29 June 1984

Dear Nick [*Hern, Methuen*],

Thank you for your letter. I must tell you that I was hurt by your leaving out Joe's dedication, because the whole romantic reason of why LOOT was a success was because, against Joe's wishes, I stamped on the Michael Codron production, and at the time promised Joe that it would be on in London in a proper production in 6 months. It was when this came to pass that Joe broke all his rules and dedicated the play to me. So it was for services rendered, not a charming gesture at all.

Love,

Dear John [*Lahr*],

After the play [*Lahr's* Diary of a Somebody, *based on the Orton Diaries*] has finished its run at the Kings Head, I would like you to remove my "character" completely. I do not want to appear on the stage, although you could use my voice on the telephone. You did not ask permission to use my character, which of course Alan Bennett and the PRICK UP YOUR EARS team did, naturally, and I will sue any theatre who subsequently perform the play with my character included. I am sure that removing me and using a telephone conversation will be satisfactory, and will not harm your play in any way.

I thought Joe turned out to be an appallingly selfish character in the play, with all the sympathy going to Kenneth, who was so feeble towards the end that one went out feeling suicidal. It is an incredibly depressing evening, which is perhaps what you wanted it to be, however all the yuppies and everybody else simply loved it, and I am sure you will make money. We have asked that our commission on the Estate's share goes to charity. I imagine AIDS would be most appropriate.

I hope you are pleased, and obviously Leonie [*Orton's sister*] is. I wonder if she realises how selfish and callous her brother appears on the stage. She was devoted to him and I certainly don't feel he <u>was</u> callous or selfish. Circumstances were beyond his control, as they were with Ken. "Beyond his control" is a line in LES LIAISONS [Dangereuses], funnily enough.

We still remain extremely beholden to you for all the critical help, and even the dubious publicity you have given to Joe. I do hope now that this is the end of all the ways of exploiting this poor dead boy. In fact I think there is nothing left to exploit, and you are so talented that I am sure you can put your talent to better service from now on.

Warm regards,

ALAN PLATER

Plater (1935–2010) approached Ramsay in 1961 at the suggestion of one of her clients, Henry Livings, who was acting in Plater's first play, which was broadcast on radio. Plater stayed with Ramsay until her death and subsequently wrote a play about her, Peggy for You, *in 1999.*

16 October 1961

Dear Mr. Plater,

Thank you for your most clear letter – one should have only North Country authors, they are such a blessing (I spent a couple of years in Rep. in Leeds, and am a great "Northern" fan).

Now, regarding an agent's ability to get a better fee, most certainly Radio is, as you know, standard. I would not be able to get you a better deal except if you wanted a particular play <u>commissioned</u> for Sound, then we would fight for a special fee.

With the BBC we always get at least £50 more for each television play. Usually we get around £350 for a first play, and if the author has two successful ones, we get them to pay around £500. Then it goes up according to how celebrated they become!

If you would prefer us to look after you right away, you could arrange for the MATING SEASON radio contract to come to us, but we won't take any commission from it, as you have written and sold it yourself, before you came to us.

Best regards,

Yours sincerely,

29 May 1962

Dear Alan,

LENNIE [Lennie's Nine Lives, *which became* A Smashing Day] is a very ambitious play which I think needs considerable revising. It is difficult to judge for the South because it is pretty harsh and awkward, whereas down here we try and pack our plays with spurious charm.

Yours ever,

15 October 1962

Dear Alan,

Any time you feel you want a play to go through "sans agent", let me know, and of course we shall take no commission but deal with it for you. When we start with an author, we are used to this kind of thing, because earnings are limited, but we find that very soon our authors earn so much money that they prefer for us to deal with everything, and the ten per cent we charge is a bit of a relief since they deduct it from their tax! I don't know why (perhaps because we can recognise talent) but as soon as authors come to us permanently, we find they earn more and more each year. I'm supposed to be "lucky" for authors, but of course my "luck" is merely their own talent, which I've been lucky enough to be allowed to handle.

I'm typing this myself, and we are in a blither of over-work – Saturdays and Mondays mail has been alarming and we are trying to clear it, with all four of us at top pressure.

Ever yours,

10 July 1964

Dear Alan,

Yes, obstructions and prevarications must be circumvented. Demand is enormous for talent, and people must not bugger it about.

Ever yours,

161

14 December 1964

My dear Alan,

The trouble about being "with it", Alan, is that this is the step before being "without it", i.e. the only place an "in" person can go, is "out". So much better to be "out" because then one might become "in". Believe me, this whole sphere of publicity and jockeying for position is pure wormwood and merely the way of people who have no proper news to discuss to fill their rag. I understand that "The Observer" has the least amount of sale of any Sunday paper. One begins to see why.

Ever yours,

30 April 1968

Dear Alan,

The West End is a money making machine, and at the moment very bad plays with very big stars are the only things that are making money or interesting the lethargic South.

Love,

Plater wrote a musical, Charlie Came to Our Town, *for the Harrogate Festival.*

6 August 1968

My dear Alan,

Harrogate seems always to me to be the only flabby town in Yorkshire. When we were in rep in Leeds we used to drive over every Sunday to the hotels for high teas, and the difference between the people living in Harrogate and Leeds is fantastic. It is a kind of pocket of the South, isn't it? In those days Trevor Howard used to be the leading man at Harrogate and Leeds and he and I were shown over the jail. I was jolly nearly detained there (this is a serious statement): I was playing a criminal lunatic in a play at Leeds, and the doctor of the jail and I were in a padded cell, and he said to me absolutely seriously, 'You can tell me the truth, you have been inside, haven't you?' I just didn't know what to say. I said 'no' but I am quite sure he didn't believe me…the people from the jail used to see all the plays.

Ever yours,

Plater was the driving force behind the establishment of the Hull Arts Centre, for which Ramsay had endowed a seat. The centre opened with his play about Hull, Don't Build a Bridge, Drain the River!, *which he told Ramsay was deliberately 'very localised'.*

[undated, 21 January 1970]

Dear Alan,

I hope the play went well last night. I should have sent you a wire, but as I wanted to write you a serious letter afterwards, I thought it sort of hypocritical to send a wire.

What I want to do is to storm a bit about your passion for documentary plays. You are so marvellously hard working with radio, TV and films, and work on them till you drop. Yet, where the theatre is concerned, you seem to prefer to take the easy road of the real-subject-background and a lot of scenes strung together, interspersed with music to jolly it up. I think that by not tackling a play – a proper play – you are doing yourself, and the theatre, a disservice.

A few years ago the playwright was dominant, because a group of playwrights, by their sheer talent, hard work and originality, turned the theatre on its head and captured it from the actors, the directors and the cliché of the well-made play. Now alas, playwrights have again gone to the bottom of the pile, and it's because most of them have taken the easy road. Above all is the miserable cliché of the documentary-with-music, based on the history of some particular town. No "unity", no attempt to make a great bridge which holds the story and the characters, just a boring set of sprightly incidents, covering as many hundreds of years as an author wishes.

It's <u>death</u> to the theatre and the playwright to continue in this way. O.K. it flatters the locale where the play happens to be set, but it doesn't begin to attempt to do anything for the theatre as a whole. It's not even difficult to do.

Of course I'm not complaining about [Close the] COALHOUSE [Door]. This was fully justified by the passion and indignation which was part of it. But I <u>don't</u> approve of your doing the documentary approach for Hull, just as I don't approve of the endless documentaries, posing as plays which come from Stoke (though they do manage to use very considerable <u>theatrical</u> skill in building them up). Practice making perfect, I suppose. Only FOR GOD'S SAKE DON'T PRACTICE?

Please write a play, for the stage, and for the stage only.

Well, I've said my say. Meanwhile I hope the Hull opening is a big success and that the notices are smashing. BUT I don't care if they ARE – it's <u>still</u> the "easy way out", and unworthy of you, dear Alan.

Love,

STEPHEN POLIAKOFF

*

At the suggestion of Christopher Hampton, the sixteen-year-old Poliakoff (1952–) sent Granny *to Ramsay.*

15 August 1969

Dear Stephen Poliakoff,

I've read what I can of your play, but I must tell you that some pages are completely blank and quite a number impossible for any of us to decipher at all. I think your photostat machine must have gone wrong. You've also got a curious kind of pagination which threw me. When I thought I was nearly at the end of Act Two, I found I was at the beginning.

Anyway, I do see what you're getting at, and I do think you have real talent for the stage, because the people come alive and I see them, hear them and understand them. The play is, of course, slight, slighter than Christopher Hampton's first play, but if James Roose-Evans wants to do it at Hampstead, I don't suppose it would do you a great deal of harm.

As you will see in the letter I wrote to Jimmie yesterday, I suggested in fun that he should commission you, but if I were you, I would resist any commission from anyone, because if you got this play on, you would earn a little money, and I think Christopher Hampton might have in mind the idea of commissioning you to write for the Royal Court, which would be by far the best thing for you, since such directors as Bill Gaskill, Lindsay Anderson and Anthony Page would be available for you there. However, if James Roose-Evans put on your first play he would try and tie you to another, but you will find that you write two or three plays before you write a really professional play with true professional merit.

Would you like to come in and have a talk to us? If so, ring up and ask Miss Leslie what time she thinks is best. You could come up to London and drop in one afternoon for tea, if you felt like it.

Kind regards,

Before Ramsay became involved, New York film and theatre producer George W. George had offered Poliakoff a commission.

22 September 1969

Dear George George,

While I am waiting for you, your lawyer, and Stephen Poliakoff to read the suggested Draft based on your offer, I want to write you a general letter about authors, so that you can know the reason for my suggestions about the Commissioned Contract you so kindly offered to Stephen.

First let me dispel your thought that I look after too many authors and that therefore Stephen can be much safer with you, as you have time for individual attention.

Over several years, I suppose we receive about five requests daily, by phone, letter or script, to look after authors which means that we could, I suppose, collect one thousand per year if we so wished!!! The fact remains that during this year we have accepted two new authors only – Nigel

Williams, an unknown at Oxford, and Stephen Poliakoff. Both of them approached us, since we never go out to "secure" authors. If we accept them, it is for their careers as a whole, and we don't do it for money; (the fact that I'd so prefer Stephen to have no commission whatever, deprives us of commission as well). In addition, we never "sign up" any author. Stephen, or anyone else, can at any time simply say they want to leave, and we would free him or anyone else.

A Manager's job is entirely different from an agent's and they are complimentary to one another. An agent's is to try and foster talent, and Stephen won't, I hope, become a Raymond Radiguet. If Cocteau had not been Radiguet's sponsor, he would certainly have had a far longer career, as his growth was exotically "forced", I feel. However, Cocteau did marvels for him, and this case is a highly debatable one, and anyone who was responsible for LE DIABLE AU CORPS can, I suppose, be forgiven for the second work being no good, and the early death of the author, who tasted the fruits of success and sophistication too early. (An interesting play should be written on the subject!).

An agent, being interested in career, longs for freedom for an author. Any commission puts him in chains, even emotional chains, because his work is "tied", and I've seen too many commissioned plays unperformed, or badly performed, and the author's career thrown for a number of years. (I should be happy to quote chapter and verse at some later date when we can discuss this matter.)

So keen am I on author's freedom, that Harbottle and Lewis are actually organising a Trust for authors, which will use the money I have earned from them in order to let them have money to write plays, should they require it, and there will be no strings attached or Contracts tied to this. When the play is written, a Manager who has already expressed an interest in the author can read the play and talk to the author about what he wants to do with it, and then he could, if he wished, repay the "Option" to the Trust. This means that a Manager will have read a play before tying it up, and he can tell the author beforehand what he wants to do, and the author is able to accept or explain that this isn't what he wants done.....

Alas, my fault isn't too many authors, it is caring too much about their talent and this does lead me to excesses of temperament and protestations.

I have no personal feelings towards them, but I do tend to be rather too passionate about talent and its development. It seems to me to be – forgive the word – something sacred.

Oddly enough, if one doesn't "claim" anything, if one does something for itself, it also happens to make one a very good living.

Best regards,

Sincerely,

Hampstead's new artistic director Vivian Matalon cancelled the theatre's plans to stage Granny *but he and James Roose-Evans came to see Poliakoff's next play,* Bambi Ramm, *which was performed at a community centre in London. They left before the third act.*

10 September 1970

Dear Jimmie,

I received a copy of your letter to Stephen, and of course you didn't have to wait till the third act to know why the play was called BAMBI RAMM, because the school-master was called Bambi Ramm and they called him that throughout the play. I understand why you say it, as you are really saying to Stephen that you didn't stay for the third act.

I think it's a very much more ambitious play than GRANNY, and because it is so much more ambitious it comes off less well. I think Stephen is trying to write about quite a private world, and his writing is totally original, and if you are discussing two kinds of plots, Stephen's is, of course, under the surface of the action.

The play seems to me very like those early writings of Cocteau, who also wrote about the private life and world of the French upper-classes and his school friends, the way Stephen is writing. Of course, Stephen needs to learn how to live, but I think he should go on writing, because I think he knows this play wasn't properly disciplined and that it was hopelessly over-written and over-long. At his age, however, it is almost impossible to impose discipline over your private world.

What I really like about Stephen is his absolute originality. He is not trying to write a well-made play, nor is he trying to write like Coward, Orton, Pinter or anyone else – he is trying to write like Poliakoff, and I think that in a few years' time when he has learned how to select and heighten, he is going to make a considerable mark.

I very much admire his character. I was incredibly tough with him after the first night, and he took it extraordinarily well. He has a lot of guts, and I am quite sure, Jimmie, that he is going to re-pay you for the interest you have taken in him from the very beginning.

It was awfully good of you and Vivian to have turned up. Actually, I found things in Act 3 extremely dramatic and disturbing, and the whole panorama of the play seems curiously real as far as I am concerned. Boring, of course, because the young are bloody boring, because they are so self-ambitious.

Love and thanks,

18 December 1970

Dear Stephen,

I've read your play [A Starting Place] and found the first twenty-four pages fresh and interesting, and then I got the oppressive Poliakoff blues, which came down on me like a blanket of boredom, and I had to fight to keep my attention on the play.

It's like the last one Stephen, you get a group of characters and then let them go on and on and on.

Your characters have charm, and one is interested for about half an hour, and then one is exhausted by them. It's like an oppressive dream from which one can't escape and which seems to go on forever.

I'm sending it back to you because you may want to show it to someone for another <u>professional</u> opinion.

I don't quite know what to advise, except perhaps, that you don't write another play until you go up to Cambridge, when you may have something to say, and you may learn how to keep our attention.

Oddly enough, this play just slightly reminds me of Dubillard's first play which I saw in Paris about eight years ago. It had great charm and for the first Act it was fascinating, and held the attention. In the second Act it just went on and on and then the curtain came down. As he was young, and the play had "flavour" it got interesting "first play" notices. Unfortunately he decided to be a professional playwright without trying to find out his weaknesses, and his plays have not been successful since. Last week a one-act play of his opened in Paris with a play by Mercer. Mercer got excellent notices I hear, but Dubillard's was slated.

A play can be slight and still hold the attention. For some reason or other, slightness isn't your problem, it's more serious – you just can't stop your characters talking and talking and it seems as if you don't really control them, or know what you want them to do. This ends up by absolutely exhausting your audience, yet at the same time puzzling them, because there is a real delicacy and fascination about the people, only you can't keep our interest in the events. As you don't know anything much about the characters, how can you develop them. I think it's basic ignorance of people and life, except the very young, which is the fault. This will be remedied with each year you live, dear Stephen, so don't <u>worry</u> about it.

Ever yours,

DAVID RUDKIN

*

Rudkin (1936–), as president of his Oxford University student drama society, had sought from Ramsay the rights to perform Ionesco's The Bald Prima Donna. *According to Rudkin, she replied: 'What are you bright young Oxford boys doing pissing around with Ionesco, for fuck's sake? Why don't you write plays of your own?' He did and sent her one in 1959, she took him on, and he stayed until her death.*

Dear David Rudkin,

One of the basic problems for playwrights is to make the ordinary extraordinary, and the extraordinary ordinary. I think humour comes with time, if one were serious altogether about life it would be insupportable.

Yours sincerely,

17 September 1962

Dear David,

I think Mann could easily quarrel and behave like a fallible human being – don't forget that he has an enormous lot to hide, even though he constantly states that all arts come from ignoble sources. But if you've never read Mann before, I beg you to break off FAUSTUS and allow me to send you a small collection of Mann in the Everyman volume – it has DEATH IN VENICE, and a bit of TONIO KRÖGER and shows clearly all his obsessions.

Mann is someone you <u>must have read</u>.

Yours ever,

8 January 1963

Dear David,

Let me know in good time when you are coming up to town again and let us arrange a proper evening for you to visit my flat, where a grand piano lies in wait for you.

Yes, I too think your association with George [*Devine*] will be something special. He's a curiously interesting man. And but for him the Court would have burst apart long ago. I always feel a bit bruised after a session with him as he's <u>rough</u>, but it's rather nice to be able to be rough back and not misunderstood. Peter Hall? Very smooth – began as a kind of doctored Tom, but much more dangerous. He wanted all the cream at the Arts but the Aldwych and the Memorial Theatre [*Stratford-upon-Avon*] have given him a taste for red meat, and he'll want human sacrifice soon.

This driving by power is a worrying affair, and I find myself rushing back to Schopenhauer in the evening. I hope you read "The World as Will and Idea". If not, please do so. Hall likes the fruits of success, silly bugger, not realising that this can't last and will destroy what creative ability he started with, leaving him <u>nothing</u>.

Yours ever,

3 May 1963

Dear David,

It's difficult for me to try and say to you that you are perhaps putting <u>yourself</u> into a kind of strait jacket of tension. The point is this: one can't, with a effort of will MAKE oneself into what one is not, or only if one does violence to oneself. Of course, one should try and choose, but one mustn't force oneself too quickly into something which after all, life itself will solve.

I think you are still too "moral" about everything. Provided one does not betray and hurt other people, it's surprising how many mistakes one can make and pick oneself up and start again. One must be <u>available for life</u>, this is the important thing. And one mustn't betray other people. For the rest, one should plunge into life easily, try and enjoy and experience all feelings and sensations and no harm need come provided one plays the game with some kind of ethical honour – never exploit or corrupt other people, that's all one needs be aware of.

Love,

2 May 1966

My dear David,

What puzzles me is your Christian standpoint, which I don't share. It seems to me that one should experience <u>everything</u>, and that a homosexual experience isn't a sin. However, if you feel you are what is quaintly called "normal" and that to succumb to a homosexual relationship might do violence to your nature and deprive you of your true sexual stand point, then of course you should not succumb.

I just don't know: we torture ourselves with this Christian stand point of "sin" – but what is sin? Provided you harm no one else, can a relationship be sinful (if the partner isn't corrupted, I mean).

You are having an appalling time wrestling, and everyone must choose his own destiny. But we are all of us in different degrees men and women – some of us are not evenly balance – not totally "man" and not totally "woman" – it's not as simple as that. Many people are both, and experience <u>both</u>. Is this violating one's nature? I don't honestly know.

Keep in touch. Try not to suffer too much. I am sure, anyway that facing this problem is necessary, and writing about it is purgative.

Affectionately, always,

16 April 1971

My dear Rudders,

I think you have been losing simplicity. I know one has to work very hard indeed for something to finally become simple, but with the recent play, you made it infinitely more complex. With my usual brashness I wrote to you at once and said that the play seemed to have been written by someone who had been exiled for twenty years in Iceland, and you replied that this was just what you wanted the play to seem!

Stanislavsky said that if one has to play a miser one must stress his generosity. You are not just clever, but revelling in it, so that you must do everything to cultivate the antithesis of your nature.

I feel sometimes David that you have lost touch with David the child, and you are living with an extremely clever, rather stuffy pompous middle-aged pedant.

Love,

9 November 1972

My dear David,

When I cease to react when I read plays, I must stop being an agent. You can't expect me not to react – the only thing I can do is not tell you.

I think both plays [The Filth Hunt *and* Atrocity] are very disturbing and the trend at the moment is to cushion people from the truth if it is unpleasant, and this is why the West End is completely unimportant and trivial – and people are flocking to see the rubbish that is being shown.

I know you stand by these plays, but if the plays are too painful, there is a possibility that they won't go on because people may be frightened. I am not trying to ask you to veil the truth, or water it down, I'm merely commenting on the fact that the plays are exceedingly painful.

Love,

WILLY RUSSELL

*

Russell (1947–) was teaching when he entered a television play competition, which he did not win, but one of the judges, Hugh Whitemore, showed the script to Ramsay, his agent. She phoned Russell and he sent her three plays, including John, Paul, George, Ringo… and Bert, *which was due to open at the Liverpool Everyman in May 1974, directed by Alan Dossor. She agreed to represent Russell and believed a London transfer, which was under discussion, might be jeopardised by a disagreement between the cast and management over wages.*

21 June 1974

Dear Alan,

Thank you for phoning, but nothing anyone can say or do will take away the sour taste.

How can one accept with indifference the spectacle of decent, good people behaving in a vulgar, grasping and mean-spirited way, simply because a play is transferring to London (the arse hole of Europe)? After all, it's only a <u>play</u>, however well done, well written, well directed and acted – it's

173

a transitory thing which will be forgotten the way every play is forgotten, and every star is forgotten and every player is forgotten. You have only to see old Cicely Courtneidge tottering into a first night, unregarded by all, to remember that once she had London at her feet and her attendance at a first night was greeted with the stalls standing up and applauding her. She earned enormous sums of money, but where are they now? The Courtneidges have to tour tatty number-three dates to pay the rent (or perhaps to sniff the smell of 'size' and hear the adrenalin-laden sound of clapping).

I understand barely 5% of the population of England go to the theatre at all; and a play is merely a mirror on life and it's not the mirror, but life itself which is important. By the same token, the actors are PLAYING the Beatles – they are not the Beatles themselves, who struggled for years, earning hardly anything finally reaching unimaginable heights only to be destroyed or destroy themselves (who knows which?)

To see decent honourable people losing their heads and grabbing for more than their share really shattered me. Nobody seemed to think that they should put more into a project than they would take out. I think the only people who have emerged from this get-rich-quick-grab-fame-and-trample-everyone-else-down-in-the-process are the Managers, and I'll add Brian [*Epstein*] who went up on behalf of McCartney, and was receptive and generous and made everything so much easier for us with no thought for himself. And, finally, Willie who I am proud to represent. He is like so many of the other authors we are lucky enough to represent – caring about their work, taking any success with a shrug, knowing that money is taxed in proportion to the earnings and finally it brings no happiness and goes in the end! The only thing worth hanging on to is one's self-respect.

So – this manifestation of an after-birth of the Beatles (not the Beatles themselves) is a sad spectacle of petty greed and ill will, attributing to Managers sordid plans for exploitation – like a couple of Simon Legrees. London Managers like Michael [*Codron*] and Bob [*Stigwood*] aren't exploiters. They care about their work, they worry about it, they do endless acts of kindness and don't make much money for themselves. Nor do they lose their heads when success comes along, knowing that the next play could well be a failure. Don't you think that the Beatles Company could perhaps get all this in perspective and try and behave like talented respected actors who care about their jobs?

Best wishes

2 July 1974

Dear Alan,

In answer to your letter, unfortunately a certain backwash of arguments fell on me both from the managerial side and from the actors' side, which greatly disturbed me.

As we have never looked after actors and hope never to do so, I am simply not used to being involved in any way with negotiations about salaries. It is very easy for an author – every detail is negotiated on paper or on the telephone, by the agent.

Just as I did not think it ethical for a director's and actor's agent to interfere with the author's negotiations, of course it is equally wrong for me to make any comment, except that I have been involved in it through no desire of my own, but by having had various people on both sides of the negotiating table (!) ring me up, and of course I am not in any position to be able to be of practical help to anybody but authors.

Anyway, I hope everything is going to go as well in London as it has been doing in Liverpool, as it's a really lovely show.

Yours,

13 September 1977

My dear Irving [*Wardle,* Times *critic*],

When are you guilt-ridden middle-class critics going to grasp that the working classes have joined the human race?

BREEZEBLOCK PARK was written by a "working-class" boy and it was written for a working-class audience, for a working-class theatre – the Everyman, Liverpool! and it was one of the greatest successes of last year – packed for weeks and weeks.

Rather foolishly, I though it a play which might be enjoyed by the South. I sold it to Tennent, but with their usual indolence they did nothing during their year. So it turned up with a Southern star which was perhaps a mistake.

The working-classes are earning just as much as the middle and upper classes. It may be that the characters in the play you saw earn more than a TIMES critic? They are quite able to laugh at criticism of themselves and their values. Just as the upper-classes were able to laugh at the criticism of themselves in Maugham's OUR BETTERS, which was about the vulgar upper-class rich.

It doesn't really matter that you don't like the play – fair enough. But why talk of 'contempt', simply because an author writes a comedy about foolish working-class ladies trying to keep up with the Joneses. It would have got an entirely different response if it had been middle-class ladies trying to keep up with the Joneses! Not contempt; perhaps satisfaction? Fair game?

All this passion for the newly rich! Well, it's a nice balance to Paul Johnson's page in last Sunday's Telegraph.

Affectionate greetings,

PS. We are in the area of Lindsay Anderson's cloth cap! (A major generals' son.)

JAMES SAUNDERS

*

Saunders (1925–2004) had just started playwriting when his agent dropped him in 1958 in response to his embrace of absurdism. Leo Lehman, a friend and client of Ramsay's, suggested Saunders try her. He was not her first client, as she claimed twenty years later, but a long-standing one who stayed with her until she died.

My dear Jimmie,

This is typed in my own fair hand, during my lunch hour when everyone is out. As you see, I've not learned to type.

As Audrey [*his wife*] will tell you, I am frightfully upset [*at a* Times *interview with Saunders*]. I've never been horrible to you, as I told her, <u>you</u> have been horrible to ME!! Now we are both bleeding, and both of us deny wounding each other, though clearly we both have done so. From my part I'm absolutely abject if I have hurt you at any time in any way, as I'm not sadistic, and never punish those I love.

Do you know you were the first author I ever looked after, and that you supported me and allowed me to look after you <u>when I started, with a borrowed £1000, absolute ignorance and no authors AT ALL</u>. You are my oldest and most valued client. Pity that this has dragged it out of me, as I'm hideously reticent and private, and wouldn't dream of burdening you with this truth, except now I feel I have to come clean.

Selfishly, I was upset because you said you earned so little, ten times less than you generally earn, because everyone in the theatre <u>will conclude that you have a totally useless agent</u>, and every agent in <u>London will be triumphant at my public disgrace</u>.

WALLACE SHAWN

*

Shawn (1943–) had written several plays when in 1975 John Lahr reviewed Our Late Night *in New York and mentioned it to Ramsay. Shawn sent her several plays. The three short plays became* A Thought in Three Parts, *which was staged in London in 1977 and was condemned in Parliament.*

10 October 1975

Dear Wallace,

You must forgive me for a fairly distraught and short letter. I don't know how it comes that we are so busy, I think it must be confusion, as busyness itself is never any excuse. We have just got a lot of plays being tried out everywhere, and it's very nerve-racking to see them, worrying about them and then trying to work out what should be done to follow.

I read THREE SHORT PLAYS several days ago and, of course, have been meaning to write. Michael Codron has them now. They are all three very interesting, but I will be surprised if we can get the middle one done as the sex is very deliberate in it!! What I mean is, the audience will accept a lot of things when a play is about a party, because everybody tends to behave rather badly at parties, and it's rather heightened living. When I say we are not likely to get it on, I mean in any decent way. We could probably give it to Michael White and Kenneth Tynan as a sequel to their Oh! Calcutta!, but I don't think that is the presentation you want. After Michael Codron has read it, I will show it to the Royal Court.

They are fearfully true plays, and very original, by that I mean people don't tell the truth in plays as a rule. Our theatre is not a mirror of life, but a weekend substitute. I really haven't more to say at the moment, so forgive me.

Best wishes,

5 December 1975

Dear Wallace,

I really enjoyed your letter of the 30 November only for God's sake stop calling me Miss Ramsay.

I have now done all my homework and I want to thank you for leading me into the rich full world of Shawn. I found the hospital play very interesting and alarming though God knows how one could get it on in England. As for the hotel play the biggest laugh is on page 98 when you say "the ideal number of actors for the play is around 75 or 80, of whom 55 (35 men, 17 women, 1 little girl and 2 little boys) must be prepared to speak a line or two!!!"

There is nothing in the least nutty about going to the Sahara Desert for a vision of truth. I spent my holiday for four years doing exactly that, and will do so again next year.

I can't go into details about the plays. I am passing them on to Hare and Brenton. I also enclose one or two tiresome letters which mustn't depress you.

It is far better to be a xerographer than a self-styled upper class complacent contributor to the New Yorker (Brendan Gill). In England Xerox machines are never on sale but on hire so that every poor devil who wants a Xerox machine has got to pay continuous rent, becoming a kind of slave to the machine, and indeed giving his life to working for Xerox. I trust you are not working on a hired machine.

Two people who are fond of one another don't really need a two-room flat – they need one room, one bed, somewhere to put books and somewhere to wash.

Affectionately yours,

16 July 1979

Dear Michael Billington [Guardian *critic*],

MARIE & BRUCE – Wallace Shawn

We are all hungry 'for the drama that offers a meaningful, developing action as well as accurate psychological reportage, for a drama that deals with wide ranging public events as well as the hermetic world of disintegrating relationships.'

However, surely there is room for the avant-garde, which this very nearly is. You would be dismissing all of Ionesco, if you felt that the only drama should be on the lines you put forward. The Theatre Upstairs is there to show all kinds of drama. Otherwise you are making a rule that only the drama you set out is permissible on the stage. Most of our authors would be 100% behind you, by the way.

Sincerely yours,

MARTIN SHERMAN

*

An American writer who was keenly interested in British theatre, Sherman (1938–) asked his New York agent in 1969 to contact Ramsay to see if she would read his plays, as he was soon to visit London. She did, over a weekend, and he remained with Ramsay until her death. He moved to London in 1980.

13 December 1987 [handwritten]

Dearest Martin,

Here is an Xmas cheque, with love.

I've so often been <u>dead broke</u> myself (and, indeed, have to <u>slave</u> to keep going, as I have a lot of responsibilities). But I was broke in the days when people <u>could</u> rescue one, quite casually, whereas now, we are all faced with finding a way to actually <u>pay our basic needs</u>.

But you mustn't despair – we are all hopelessly struggling to keep alive, you know, and we understand each other's crises, and <u>care</u> about them.

Fondest love,

COLIN SPENCER

*

Spencer (1933–) was a short story writer, novelist, and artist when he joined Ramsay in the mid-1960s as a playwright.

29 November 1971

Dear Colin,

THE TRIAL OF SAINT GEORGE

I am absolutely delighted by the German reaction to the Little Claws, which will entirely change the German attitude towards pricks. I imagine perhaps it will lower the birth rate.

Obviously this is a man's play, and they like to think of their pricks as dragons. I am just wondering if it is a woman's play, even those butch Germans.

Anyway, it will be lovely to see, and I am so pleased for you.

Love,

JOHN WHITING

*

Ramsay came to represent Whiting (1917–63) when in 1958 she formed Peters and Ramsay, linking with the literary agent A. D. Peters, whose own firm concentrated on and represented many of the leading novelists. She inherited a number of writers from Peters, including J. B. Priestley and Whiting. Peters had little to do with the new firm, which brought in no new talent, and Ramsay closed it in 1971. After Whiting's death at the age of forty-five, a playwriting award was established in his name.

24 April 1961 [handwritten]

Dear John,

Much of the book [The Inner Experience of a Psychoanalyst *by Theodore Reik*] is tedious and rambling, but embedded in it is some interesting material for the writer. For instance, he says, "As a rule we experience an event a long time after its occurrence. In many cases the interval is so long that the causal connection is quite lost to us. This ignorance, <u>which is to some extent a will to ignorance</u>, implies a protective measure on the part of the mind for, if we knew, we should not be equal to receiving the knowledge. To experience

181

means to master an impression inwardly that was so strong that we could not grasp it at once."

"While conscious we see only the subject, unconscious we see also our own selves within the subject. The comprehension of another is a transformation of the ego, the <u>becoming another</u>. We have devoured our subject, and so have wholly become the subject."

Finally: "A man's unconscious self also contains possibilities of his life that were lived only in the imagination, <u>potentialities of his destiny that never become real</u>. There are mysterious repetitions in the choice of similar objectives of love, puzzling resemblances in failure and success, friendships broken up under the same circumstances, affairs that take the same developments along with seemingly quite unexpected interludes that show the reverse side. There are necessary 'life lies' that go hand in hand with a clear understanding of the truth; tenderness that is only the cover for cruel action; and cruel actions that hide affectionate feelings."

"It is not the dream itself in its interpreted, deciphered meanings, but the thoughts out of which the dream is born, the emotional raw material and the way the dreamer uses them, the special twists and turns he gives them, that are significant and present precious clues to the analyst about the character of the dreamer."

"The Ego is the last Dark Continent."

Yours,

11 April 1961 [handwritten postcard]

"A man can do anything in the world if he doesn't mind not getting the credit for it...the more you are talked about, the less powerful you are." <u>Beaconsfield</u> [Disraeli].

25 April 1961 [handwritten postcard]

"To heal all things, wretchedness, disease or the melancholy, absolutely nothing is required but an inclination for work." (Baudelaire) "Every defeat of the will forms a portion of lost matter. How wasteful is hesitation! One may judge this by the immensity of the final effort necessary to repair the losses." (Baudelaire).

3 May 1961

Dear John,

I'm now reading REALISM AND IMAGINATION, a rather dreary book by [*Joseph*] Chiari (dreary because one agrees with him most of the time). One sentence, however, struck my eye.

"Artistic greatness is measured by the degree of impersonality which is also universality." Now [*this*] is obvious, but surely it's awfully controversial to say that our "characters" are masks hiding the truth? I agree that people's interpretations of our characters are pretty certain to be false, but do we, in fact, cover ourselves with a false outer covering? We of course conceal, but do we consciously give false indications in order to put people off the scent? And do we self-deceive, consciously?

P.S. I've just had time to read the first 11 pages [*of Whiting's* The Gates of Summer, *seen briefly in 1956 in Oxford*] – cold, cruel, enigmatic, literary – <u>so</u> far – I expect I'll settle down.

Yours,

4 May 1961

Dear John,

I continue to record my crude white hot feelings regarding GATES OF SUMMER. Everything I say is based on instinctive emotion and is therefore exaggerated and unsound.

Yet by judging a play personally, unguardedly, "on the hoof" as it were, one might possibly find one or two valid points. However, I hope you won't dread hearing from me and that I'm not being too impetuous and tactless.

Anyway, I've finished Act One. Those characters of yours are so "civilized", so articulate and so sophisticated but they've cut themselves off from the deepest fountains of their beings – everything seems to be "from the head".

Yours,

8 May 1961

Dear John,

I took the play [The Gates of Summer] to Cambridge and made notes in the night, but find I must have left my scribblings at the Garden House [*hotel*].

To sum up: the impact of THE DEVILS has been so tremendous, that everyone will turn up with high hopes, and you simply cannot afford to take a backward step, now that you have won the race. I don't mean that you must write serious epics, but I do complain of much of the triviality of the action; it's as if you aren't taking your audience seriously.

This play is brilliantly written, with splendid things in it, but every play, surely, should be as if the author is saying his "last words", as if you were whispering marvellous secrets into the ears of the audience which you might forget unless you told them these things (now, at once – Whitman's secret!).

I don't expect you agree with these reflections, and as they are personal they are, certainly, suspect.

Yours, in haste,

29 December 1961

Dear John,

When you become invulnerable, you'll cease to be John Whiting, and I hope that doesn't happen in our lifetime. How the <u>ordinary</u>, well balanced citizen manages to live life is astounding, but those who have imagination are bound to nearly break from time to time – there's only one word anyone can give to anyone else and that's "<u>Endure</u>".

Yours, in great haste,

CHARLES WOOD

*

Wood (1932–) had two television plays and one for radio to his credit but none for the stage when the agency that represented him closed in 1962. His friend Peter Nichols suggested Wood approach Ramsay, his agent. Having heard the radio play, she agreed to represent Wood.

Friday [undated, 22? May 1964]

My dear Charles,

Glad you enjoyed [Entertaining] MR SLOANE. Rattigan wrote a great fan letter to the author and has offered to put up £5000 to get the play done in the West End. It won't be a hit I fear as it's a "special audience" play I think. In a weak moment I was dragged into backing the play and have to contribute the same sum again if it transfers. I've lost every time at the Arts and will do the same in the West End. I'm not sour, but Michael [*Codron*] doesn't back his own plays and merely takes his managerial fee for every week it plays, so no wonder he doesn't mind transferring…anyway it's nice to hear an agent losing money on an author every now and then!!!

Personally I didn't see ANY Mods or Rockers at Brighton [*where she was about to buy a house*]. I must decide which side I'm on by next Bank Holiday so that I too can break up a few deck chairs and do a bit of damage. You and Peter [*Nichols*] can cheer me on. I'd love to do a bit of destruction and don't really get a proper chance. I DO so sympathise with the kids over this, and think we should have adult factions and go out weekly and bust up districts. Eaton Square, for instance [*the London area where Ramsay had a flat*], or Buck House.

Your letter sounds as if you're working far too hard. It hurts. I'm being specially slack at the moment and can hardly bring myself to read a play, and the office is something I detest. However the rest of the boys and girls seem to be specially devoted to their work, thank god.

185

Haven't heard a peep out of P. Nichols. I suppose he's decorating his hearth.

I'm going up to see the Soviet play at Oxford next Wed [The Twelfth Hour *by Alexei Arbuzov, translated by Ramsay's client Ariadne Nicolaeff*]. Has a sweet little author. Specially nice that we can't communicate!!

It's six so I'm buggering off for the week-end.

Love,

30 December 1964 [handwritten]

Well, yes, Charlie baby, an hour [*of* Last Summer by the Seaside, *Wood's TV programme on English holidays*] is a bit too long to be art-less and plot-less. However I napped cosily from time to time and each time I woke up <u>there</u> was the Wood family in coloured knickers having a whale of a time. The trouble was that <u>they</u> were enjoying themselves more than I was. Next time I shall hope that <u>you</u> are doing the suffering and that <u>I</u> am doing the enjoying!

However, a nice little programme and it will certainly give your public a false feeling of your <u>ordinariness</u>, as opposed to the Charles Wood WE know!

Love,

Wood left Ramsay in 1976.

14 January 1976

Dear Charles,

You couldn't write for money if you tried – you are a dedicated writer. I wish you great good fortune.

As for private letters and private matters – I've been approached by most of the publishers and some agents asking me to write a book and I have always replied that one couldn't tell the truth in a book, as it would be misinterpreted.

I will certainly write about the theatre at some future date but I won't descend to including personal letters and personal anecdotes. I've seen too many good writers' letters, like Conrad's and Kipling's, complaining about their agents and publisher's (for God's sake) which simply make me sad that people of this calibre can stoop to petty vindictiveness – particularly Conrad: who would have <u>thought</u> it?

Ever yours,

*

Before becoming an agent, Ramsay read plays for several managements. In February 1953, she wrote to Rex Frost, the author of one of the plays she had read. She represented him when she became an agent, and his play, The Jolly Fiddler, *was produced in Liverpool. It later transferred to London, in October 1955, retitled* Small Hotel.

5 February 1953

Dear Mr Frost,

You will not know me, but I am "reader" for Reandco, and in that capacity I read your play and liked it very much.

I have been meaning for a long time to ask them if they intend to take it or if they have rejected it. Meanwhile I'm writing to you to ask you the news about it, and if it is still "free", as I would like to recommend it, if you would allow me (not as an agent of course, simply as an admirer).

Yours sincerely,

Edward Sutro was among the first people to support Ramsay in setting up as an agent.

Thursday [undated, late 1953]

My dear Edward,

I can see that the real headache is going to be saying "No" to so-so plays – all of them must be sales worthy, so that we can build up a really first class reputation.

Love,

Dear Mr [*Toby*] Rowland,

Thank you so much for your letter, and may I wish you every possible success in management.

It is difficult for me to know what play to send you because I don't know exactly what your policy is going to be. Of course you are looking for good plays, but should they be basically commercial, or would you put on <u>any</u> play, provided it was really remarkable?

If you are capable of folly, I'd like you to read a young Cambridge graduate's translation of "Danton's Death" – a superb play by Büchner, which Orson Welles did in New York with great réclame, but which I have not had the temerity to offer any London manager. I showed it to the Third Programme and they have just offered us a production in July. It is remarkably translated [*by John Holmstrom*], but needs adaptation modifications which could be done in consultation with a producer. Welles cut a number of the small parts, for instance.

Another possibility is that you might be interested in one of Leo Lehman's plays. He is a young man who the Arts Council have granted £500 bursary, as the most outstanding and promising young playwright they have come across. I've just had one of his comedies "Home and Continental" tried out at Sheffield for two weeks and it played to packed and enthusiastic houses. I sent a script to Frith Banbury, who has asked to meet the author, but has not made an offer for the play as yet. He has also written a five hander set in the Pacific called The Innocent Volcano. I've not sent the play to anyone in England except Murray Macdonald who told me he thought it tremendously good, but did not dare to do it himself. It is going on in Vienna quite soon.

If you are not too busy and can spare the time, do come in for a cup of tea and a talk, and then I can know exactly what you are looking for. I "read" for several London managers as well as running this firm, so I know most of the plays going the rounds and will gladly recommend those I think good, for what it's worth.

Yours sincerely,

Iain Mackintosh co-founded Prospect Productions in 1961. Whiteman by Ramsay's client Michael Picardie was the first play it staged.

12 September 1961

Dear Iain Mackintosh,

Thanks for your letter – your Sunday typing is better than my Tuesday's… as you see!

The first lesson to be learned in the theatre is to <u>endure</u>.

Don't despair. Remember that Binkie started H.M.T. [*Tennent*] with a series of dead flops, he opened the Lyric Ham[*mersmith*] to empty houses; Codron laid an egg first time; Toby Rowland is still doing so! Actually one learns more from this kind of thing than a tremendous success – one must prepare oneself for that, it's most destructive and disconcerting, and it should really only arrive when you have ceased to care whether it comes or not!

Warm good wishes,

25 October 1963

Dear Miss [*Sheila*] Lemon [*a new agent*],

I've been at this job for nearly nine years now and it's a heart breaking job and almost an impossible job to do well, and one is bound to fail in the end, because one is, after all, living on other people's talents, and this in itself requires the utmost humility and an acceptance of what is sometimes pretty rough behaviour from the talented ones! There is no doubt at all that had I known the horrors of the job, nothing would have induced me to become an agent.

I know how tough it is to begin with, because I began with no money and no authors, and no money I've made since (and we've made a lot) can recompense me for the miseries and pressures we've suffered in the process. Everything has to be paid for, and the price is always too high.

Good wishes,

Sincerely yours,

Dear Ken [*Tynan*],

Hobson phoned to ask me what was wrong with our theatre. I wonder if you, in your fastness, can diagnose? My own feeling is that it is being choked by the middle-men, the exploiters, the agents, the reporters, the editors, the script-editors, the TV producers, the readers etc. etc. To every actually "creative" person, there are a dozen living off him, or wanting to write about him, or to get him to lecture, or appear on TV. This great lazy, exploiting body of untalented people are choking the life out of show-biz.

I hope you're having fun [*as Literary Manager of the National Theatre*] and don't miss THE OBSERVER [*for which he had been a celebrated theatre critic*] as much as we miss you.

Love,

17 April 1964

Dear Anthony [*Page, a director*],

I am exhausted and fed up. This life has such pressures and I'd like to escape altogether – it isn't <u>living</u>, is it?

Stuart Gilman, a Canadian playwright living in London, corresponded with Ramsay for a year while she tried in vain to sell his plays.

13 May 1965

Dear Stuart,

Of course I realise you need money, but your plays aren't sellable at the moment, and I don't honestly think that you can hope to earn anything from your plays at the moment. Most of our highly talented authors began by having jobs which supported them until they were able to earn sufficient from their writing. I know this is a method which doesn't appeal to you, but the alternative is a kind of blackmail. I know there is a school of thought, to which I used to subscribe, that the world owes an artist a living. I am not absolutely sure about this anymore. I think all of us have to do unpleasant things, and I think all of us should carry our own responsibilities, as far as this is possible. I don't think that certain members of the community should support other members of the community, just because they happen to be artists. There is probably an area of artist in every human being, and the important thing is to try and see that one gives sufficient of one's life to creativity, so that it is not smothered or withered. On the other hand, gifts and loans don't particularly help an author, I can assure you. This is the quickest way to become a bum. I am surprised to find myself writing a letter of this sort, I always used to drool over authors, and have, indeed, been known to give them money. However, no good has ever come out of this. I should much prefer not to work from 10am to 6pm, in order to enlarge upon the latent capacities I have myself, and I am sure there are a number of stock-brokers who have a seed of strong creativity in them.

The real trouble with writing for the theatre is to find people who have both talent and character. The snag about loans and gifts is that it results in corroding character.

Nobody ever wrote me this kind of letter when I was bumming around Hampstead, but I rather wish they had.

Ever yours,

Dear Stuart,

I am very glad that you are tackling this whole problem of step by step events in a play. I don't think it is your self-centredness or your youth. I think you just find you have not been given this talent for story-telling, and for this very reason you must practice it. The professional writer Maugham was unable to do "descriptions" and in his note-book it is awfully touching to see the hundreds of attempts he made, and how in the end he managed very well.

There is that standard book on Drama [Dramatic Technique] by [*George Pierce*] Baker, which I could try to get you from America, but in a way it isn't just that. Why not write me a little story with a beginning, a middle and an end – quite childish if you like using your characters to meet one another, and the consequences of their meeting, say. This problem of storytelling doesn't have to be built into a play to begin with – you need to be able to tell a story. You will have to learn to do this. Even Proust managed it, by living it! However, I don't suggest you take 40 years to tell one story! If I were you I should try one or two "tales" a la Maupassant. You do them and I will criticize. Don't criticize yourself, or you will never write them.

Have you tried re-writing some of the stories of Chekhov? He does plots by series of irrelevancies, as it were. What you need to do is to borrow our volumes of Ibsen and synopsize them, i.e. make a little plan showing what each scene contains, and how it links to the next, and how the whole thing is a total theme. If you would like to come and collect some Ibsen you are welcome to do so.

Yours ever,

19 October 1965

Dear Audrey Wood [*a grande dame of US agents, whom Ramsay respected*],

I don't think I will come to America this year. At the moment our theatre is in bad shape, and we have nothing but minor playwrights fully satisfied with themselves. It seems to me that all of us should be working hard to get better playwrights stretching themselves further. Over here we are all busy taking things out of the theatre and putting little there. I think I would be better spending the rest of this year finding new talent and developing it. Our promising new authors appear to have been spoilt from the beginning and are not developing – they are so darned satisfied with themselves! This makes our theatre boring and uninteresting. If we can't make it better than this we ought not to be in this metier.

Warmest regards,

A new play by Günter Grass, The Plebeians Rehearse the Uprising, *excited interest in the UK, including from Columbia Pictures, during its*

rehearsals in Berlin. Ramsay represented Grass's stage work in the UK at this time.

11 November 1965

Dear John [*Van Eyssen, Columbia Pictures*],

The German agent sounds a little too excited and pleased with the play for safety. I like authors and agents to be near suicidal before a play opens, don't you agree?

Warmest regards,

Yours,

21 December 1966

My dear Irving [*Paul Lazar, US agent*],

WE CROSS THE RUBICON AT DAWN

I know Theodore White's extremely high reputation as a journalist, but I couldn't possibly represent this play. I think it's a great hollow rhetorical windbag of a play, full of "fine writing", over-inflated sentiments, old-fashioned, ranting and boring, boring, boring.

Of course, some other agent might be prepared to take on this kind of thing, but I couldn't show this play to anyone and keep a straight face.

Do get other opinions, but for God's sake ask people who aren't afraid of telling the truth. I'll be delighted to be proved entirely wrong, as it would give me the greatest pleasure for you to have a big success in the theatre.

Love from,

The Royal Court staged Insideout *by Frank Norman [1930–80], an autobiographer and novelist who had come to prominence as a playwright with Joan Littlewood's 1959 production of* Fings Ain't Wot They Used T'Be.

Dear Mr. Norman,

I only read your New Statesman article yesterday, so I am well behind the times in my reaction.

You must forgive me if I write you a personal letter, as you won't know who I am. So – I'd better say that I am an agent for playwrights. This means I was specially interested in your letter, and specially shocked that you should have written it.

As far as playwrights are concerned, their object is to become professionals, and develop careers. The people I represent, and you would probably recognise many of their names, all started totally unknown, and slowly, with the years, they have become able to earn their living in the theatre, radio, films and television. They are in a word, <u>professionals</u>, and professionalism is, as you know, the combination of talent, industry and character.

In any profession one has one's successes and failures, and one usually learns more from one's failures. After a time it's really the development of the talent that matters, and the words "failure" or "success" become meaningless.

I know how bloody awful it is to have a play on and be savaged by the critics, but criticism isn't really very important. Chekhov had pretty bloody awful criticism to begin with, both in Russia and in England, and he had productions, one finds, when one reads his private letters, which he personally detested. But I don't think he ever wrote to the Moscow papers complaining!

Would you honestly have written to the Staggers [*New Statesman*] had you been praised by the critics? Would you have written to say that your success was entirely due to Lindsay [*Anderson*] and Anthony [*Page, Artistic Directors of the Royal Court*]? And, do you think that Lindsay and Anthony deliberately tried to hurt your play? Of course you know that a play is a <u>blueprint</u> for performance, which is why the theatre is so difficult and why everything seldom comes together for good.

I'd heard that Lindsay was responsible for having your play done in the first place – certainly we'd hoped that a play by one of our clients would fill the dates given to your play. Fair enough, we thought, marvellous that someone as talented as you should come into the theatre and be given priority. But how sad to read that it ended in recrimination and hate!

Lindsay Anderson is a remarkable and outstandingly talented man. Difficult, ruthless, single-minded, as most outstandingly talented people become. This is a form of protection without which talent can't survive. Have you any idea how many "failures" Lindsay had to endure, and how he lived through them, and continue to work? Okay, not everything *succeeds*, perhaps he can't interpret everything, who can? Perhaps your play would have been better if left to Mr [Ken] Campbell [the director], but do you honestly think that Lindsay and Anthony were thinking of themselves when they came in and did what they did? So, the play didn't "come off". So what the hell? Is "success" important? Surely what is important is the development of your talent and your career as a whole? An article such as you wrote, doesn't hurt the theatre who put on your play, or the Directors who tried to help. It ends by hurting you, and I'm sorry about this.

Do continue to write for the theatre, but don't let an odd production which doesn't "please" you, set you back. For God's sake live through it, take it as part of the game. You have plenty of guts for life, why not show some guts about your profession as a playwright?

If I gave you a list of "successful" plays which appeared during the last few years – those praised by the critics and supported by thousands of playgoers, you wouldn't remember the names of the authors. What, for instance, has become of N.C. Hunter? All his plays ran for years at the Haymarket, and the poor bugger is now stranded on the island of his past success, utterly forgotten, and a sad and embittered man. I met this ghost at a party a few years ago, and he asked me to read one of his "new" plays. He was still writing "sub" Chekhov. He hadn't learnt a thing from all his success.

Sincerely yours,

5 August 1971

Dear Tom Courtenay,

I must say, I should hate to be a casting director, because actors seem to be imprisoned in impregnable fortresses, which is perhaps as it should be!

Best wishes,

Dear Sir Cecil [*Beaton*],

OF THE COMPANY

I enjoyed reading your play, and I have talked to a number of Managers about what chance there might be of yet another production, and the chances seem slim indeed.

Even though you had two productions you found lamentable, the publicity, because of your name, must have been enormous and everyone in the theatre seems either to have seen it, or had reports on it.

I can't help feeling that it would be advisable for someone of your eminence not to have a play hawked around and at the end of it find a not sufficiently good Manager to agree to do it.

My own views on its chances are not very hopeful, though I found the story of Gainsborough very interesting, and you have a definite dramatic flair.

I didn't approve of the interpolated songs, because you were writing a straight play and suddenly expected the whole thing to stop and have the straight actors burst into melody. The only place I thought it legitimate was at the end of Act One Scene One. Nor did I approve of the racy language which I somehow found distracting – "Having a ball", to look "chipper" and "Worry her not" forsooth!

What a pity you have already written your memoirs, because as I was reading the play I kept thinking WHY doesn't he write about his own life and times. Have you thought about this from a theatre point of view? For instance, adolescence and young manhood.

All good wishes and I hope you don't mind my giving you gratuitous advice.

Sincerely,

Dear Michael [*Codron*],

I don't really know whether I'm right to drop you a note about that profile of you in the Sunday Times, or simply accept that we are now going separate personal ways.

The 'Fringe' which no longer interests or even rates your presence, is the reflection of the "have nots" – the young, the aspiring, the critical, the brave, the writers of the future….the commercial theatre is the "haves" – middle class, middle brow, privileged, indifferent to anyone who "<u>has not</u>".

The admirable thing was that you, yourself, set out your supposed limitations. John Gale doesn't even <u>think</u> about it – he puts on plays for money and for the backers' delight…and to fill the theatre with mindless, thoughtless, careless people. As long as they pay what does he care?

This ossification which you accept is the ossification which destroyed Rattigan; there he was, with money, success, an elite group of yes-men… and he was left behind.

Well, we all come full circle, unless we are determined to renew ourselves each day and to live as far as possible with those who <u>have</u> to use the tube, the bus, the cafe…

When I read your reference to RING FOR CATTY [*his first West End venture*] I knew where I stood…<u>outside</u> your "money-is-success" group. But, thank God, I've <u>not</u> been seduced by rubbing shoulders with the few "successful" authors we represent. I respect and like them, and am grateful to them (and of course I'll send you their new plays), but I don't let them shrink my tastes, and don't even think <u>they</u> want to be labelled "West End", and I don't think you are doing <u>them</u> a good turn by saying you like them but don't like the experimenters; they would all be quite happy to write for the "Fringe". (I speak for "our" authors who don't think the West End the be-all of their careers anyway).

We started together with nothing, and you will end with lots of money and lots of success. I hope I will end with <u>nothing</u> except my respect for unknown talent.

Love,

P.P.S.

*

Dear Henry [*Popkin, US critic and academic*],

It IS tempting to represent such giants as Pirandello and Brecht and the rest...For my part, I like my authors alive, and I strive to keep them that way, if I can,

Ever yours,

WWW.OBERONBOOKS.COM

13 August 1964

Dear Alan;

Im typing this myselr with a heavy cold, so both hands
and head will probably let me down!

Im so glad you feel encouraged by this idiotic peter
Bridge affair - he is, as you know, totally talentless, and
I tried to warn you. I dont in the least feel you to be
"unmanageable", and indeed want to cheer you up and
encourage you. My only concern is that you dont too often
caricature human beings rather than characterise them . i.e.
do strip cartoons rather than picutres! Id love you to do
a few sketches for the new Michael White Eoeanor Fazan
revue - jot anything down and Ill arrange for you to meet
her for a talk. Id also like yo to think about writing a
comedy for television. Are you interested in writing for TV?
Id imagine you could write a good play for that medium.

If you want to come and have a tlak any time , just
phone and make a date. Im always pleased to see you and am
very anxious to start you on something else.

I must go and have a good blow!

Love,